# 7 More Speeches
## on the sacredness of the female

The Honorable Minister Louis Farrakhan

# ACKNOWLEDGEMENTS

The Final Call Foundation humbly acknowledges the labor of the members of the ministry class of Muhammad's Temple No. 7 in New York, New York and the believers who assisted them in various capacities to publish the book, "7 Speeches by Minister Louis Farrakhan" in 1974.

That book is the inspiration for this one.

# CONTENTS

# EDITOR'S NOTE

The edited transcripts of these seven lectures
are marked with subheadings to facilitate the careful study
of the words of the Honorable Minister Louis Farrakhan.

# 1 THE BLACK WOMAN

*As-Salaam Alaikum!* In The Name of Allah Who came in the Person of Master Fard Muhammad, the One God to Whom All Praise is Due, the Lord of the Worlds. We thank Almighty God Allah for blessing us, the Black man and Black woman of America, with a divine leader, a divine teacher and a divine guide, the Honorable Elijah Muhammad.

My beloved Brothers and Sisters, we thank you for honoring us with your presence this evening. We are honored that you took time from your schedule to pay us a visit. We have been looking for you and we are happy that you choose this particular evening to come. Now that you are here, some of you for your first time, we want to welcome you home, as this is your home. We want you to know that every time the doors open, this is where you should be.

Any party that is going on—you know, we love to groove it. We want to know, where is the party? We want to know, where is the happening that we may go and help it happen. This is where the party is, and this is where the happening is. So, this is where you should be. Usually there is some theme at a party—a birthday party, a wedding anniversary party, a smoking reefer at the party—there's always something at the center around which everybody parties.

Here, we party around wisdom. We believe that you are going to enjoy this party more than you have enjoyed any party that you have attended, especially when we take up with you the type of subject that we are taking up with you—the Black woman. It must have caught your ear: the Black woman.

The temple is packed from the top all the way to the bottom. The classrooms are filled, the basement auditorium is filled. They are watching on closed circuit television. We are glad to see you. I am so happy to see you, I don't know whether I should begin my subject. I could stand and just look at you. You are beautiful. You are beautiful.

## Wise generations

To get acquainted with each other, we begin to see the beauty in each other. We fall in love with each other. When the Black man falls in love with his Black self, then the enemy gets mighty worried. White people don't mind a Black man getting knowledge. They don't mind you getting smart because when you get smart, an individual gets smart. But they don't want to see a smart Black woman in the right way because when she gets smart, a nation gets smart. A man is important. He's important but look at how important the woman is.

He will educate you, but if he can keep her dumb, he's got you. In all your smartness, he keeps you busy out in the world trying to make a living, while your dumb woman is bringing your dumb babies into the world. She is their first teacher. Solomon said it so beautifully [Proverbs 10:1]: "A wise child maketh a glad father but a foolish child is the heaviness of its mother." This is to show you how important the woman is. If the woman is allowed to be foolish, she is going to make a foolish generation. You and I don't teach the babies. She is their teacher. If we are wise men, we want our women, not to be smart, we want them to be full of wisdom. Then, we have a wise nation coming up.

## Elijah Muhammad's classroom

The enemy will go to any length to keep you away from the Honorable Elijah Muhammad, you [Black women]:

*"If your husband comes, well that's alright but don't you get*

*near Muhammad. He's a hate teacher. He's trying to make slaves of women. He's a male chauvinist. He doesn't believe in women's liberation or even women's rights. He wants to just make you ugly and unattractive."*

*"He doesn't want us to exercise our talents. He wants to keep us bound in the house. We hate Muhammad. Our silly husbands can love him, but we don't want nothing to do with that man. Just give us Moses and Jesus and the rest of their prophets."*

This is the way he is going after us. He has the house divided against itself. It was already divided, now it's more divided. He is a pretty smart man but not smart enough. If he had thought that you would be here tonight—this kind of sight makes him sick. Now, I want to go to work so I can make him sicker.

I want to remind you and acquaint you with the teacher of the classroom. The teacher is Elijah Muhammad. He's the only man fit and worthy to head a classroom full of Black people. He's not a man with theories. He's not a man of guesswork. He is a man who knows. I am proud to be one of his students and I know that I am standing in his classroom. Therefore, I don't want to make a mistake so that I may discredit my teacher. I don't want to discredit him. I want to honor him. The only way I can honor Muhammad is to teach you properly what he has taught me. So, it's not I who is teaching actually; it is Muhammad teaching. It is Farrakhan reciting what he heard the teacher say.

We are not used to listening to a Black teacher. In fact, Black teachers have really had nothing to say to us but what White people taught them. Generally, the Black professor was a professor of white teaching so he never could better the condition of the Black man.

But in Elijah Muhammad, we have a God-raised and God-taught man. *[recording skips]* Allah (God) is the Best Knower. To know means to have knowledge, and to have knowledge is to be acquainted

3

with facts. To have the facts is to have that upon which to build successfully. If The Best Knower is the Teacher of Elijah Muhammad on the Black woman, Black man, and the Time and what must be done, then you will never find a teacher of knowledge who will give you one-eighth, 1/100, 1/1000 about the knowledge that I am about to impart to you about yourself.

This is how mighty Muhammad is as a teacher. What he is about to say to you through me this evening, I want you, my Brothers and Sisters, to weigh it, look into it, and I think we will even have a question series for you to question it. This is the only place that you can go that you can listen to somebody say what they want to say, and we don't tell you to take it on face value. Question it. And when you're satisfied, accept it.

## Blackness and the first atom of Life

We're talking about the Black woman. How is she Black? Why don't we talk about the White woman? Why not talk about the Yellow woman? Why not talk about the Brown woman? Why should we make our subject the Black woman? Who is she? What kind of woman is she? What is her nature?

I think we better bring the [chalk]board. If it gets a little warm, just open the windows. We're not going to be here very long, but we hope to be here very strong, very strong. Brothers, I don't mean to turn the board away from you, but my Sisters are over here.

Why are we talking on the Black woman and why is she Black? Her blackness tells you something about her age. If she was a recent creature, she would not enjoy the same blackness of skin as the Originator and the Original Man.

Messenger Muhammad teaches us that the first atom of life represents God Himself. That first atom of life, Messenger Muhammad teaches, is a Self-Created atom. It is not something that has a mother or father. It is something that is self-created. Muhammad teaches us that the first atom of life came forth in a universe of total triple darkness—meaning darkness upon darkness upon darkness, layers of darkness. As the Bible and Holy Qur'an teach, light did not come first. Light came after darkness, and light came out of darkness. Darkness preceded light. Darkness is the essence, not only of light but of life. It all came out of darkness.

Talking on the Black woman. She's something. To know her is to know you, and to know you is to know her, because you are both part of the same and, in reality, are the same. You can never function properly until you are one.

Messenger Muhammad said to us that the first atom of life built itself up in total darkness into light. Not that it was light, but it was the atom of life. That atom had to start from water because water is the base of life, but that water was in total darkness.

Messenger Muhammad said that the atom of life is the base or the essence—but as it built itself up into light, it evolved in darkness. It evolved in darkness. It evolved. In darkness, it was in motion, it was moving.

He teaches us that our blackness is not because we were something of a divine curse. The blackness of our skin is to show that we were the first life out of the total blackness of a darkened universe. Being the first life out of the blackness of space, we took our pigmentation from the environment out of which we emerged. Therefore, the first life, the Original Life, the Original Man is referred to as the Black man.

Look at your Black face and rejoice, Brothers and Sisters. I know what White folks told you that because you are Black, you are nothing. But look again at your beautiful Black face. Look at that beautiful Black face, Sisters. Why are you beautiful? You were the first. You are absolutely the God.

## Woman: The first part of God

If the Originator came out of blackness and took the pigmentation of His skin from the environment of blackness out of which He emerged, Messenger Muhammad said He could not continue His own life except by creating from Himself that through which He could continue to reproduce Himself. Therefore, the scripture never says, "Let me make man." Muhammad teaches this is the impossibility even with God. It says [Genesis 1:26], "and God said, 'Let Us make man.'" Remember that.

The Creator created all life to die. That's a law: Every living thing must die. Then, that first Life that created Itself would also die. But He gave Himself that through which He could reproduce Himself again and again and again and again.

If the God saw the need in the very beginning, billions of years ago before the sun, moon, and star, to reproduce His Own Self through a part of Himself that He got from Himself, then the Black woman is the first part of God. She is that part of the God through which God reproduces His Own Self.

The Black woman is no plaything, Brother. All life bears witness to the Messenger's teaching. Mr. Muhammad said look how Allah (God) makes all life bear witness to His beginning. Mr. Muhammad says no life starts in the light. All life gets its beginning in total blackness.

## The unity of the body

All life begins in total blackness as a tiny drop of water or a tiny drop of blood. That's it. Yet from one cell, all life begins to evolve in blackness, starting to move. Look how we evolve in the darkness of our mother's womb—not in the light but in the dark from one cell. How many cells are in the human body? Billions of cells. How many cells did you start from?

If you started from one and yet you have multiplied into billions, are those billions any different from the one? No. All that is in the billions is found in the one. Those billions in unity are an extension of the power of one. I'm not going to let you sleep. This is one class where nobody sleeps.

We all started from one cell and the universe and Allah (God) Himself started from one atom. The universe is composed of billions of atoms, all of them in oneness. Black people don't trace our ancestry back to Africa. We don't trace our ancestry back to South America. We don't trace our ancestry back to Asia. We trace our ancestry back beyond the sun, moon, and star to that first atom of Life Who created Himself in the blackness of space. Our beginning was with the beginning of God Himself.

# 2 RESPECT FOR WOMANHOOD

In The Name of Allah, The Beneficent, The Merciful. I bear witness that there is no God but Allah and that Muhammad is His Messenger. Brothers and Sisters, it is once again my great privilege and pleasure to have this opportunity to share with you some of that which we have learned as a result of our study of the Qur'an and the Bible under the guidance of the Teachings of the Honorable Elijah Muhammad. I am very pleased to be back with you again after being absent from you for about two or three Sundays. I want to pay a special thank you to Sister Ava Muhammad for her representation of Islam and the Teachings of the Honorable Elijah Muhammad.

I think many, particularly our Muslim Brothers and Sisters abroad, may wonder why we should utilize women in speaking the Words of Allah, and is this a departure from the Qur'an. Is this a departure from the sunnah of Prophet Muhammad, peace be upon him (PBUH). Prophet Muhammad as I understand him was a great liberator of women.

As I understand him, Prophet Muhammad came among the Arabs at a time of great disrespect of womanhood, where the female young were being buried alive and where women were disrespected. Unfortunately, if Prophet Muhammad were to reappear, he would have to set women free again. Women are enslaved in 1986 by false concepts of self, false concepts that have been advanced mostly by men of religion who for one reason or another misunderstand the place of women in the work of Almighty God. The Holy Qur'an which is the book of scripture of the Muslims and righteous people, always refers to "the believing men and the believing women, the charitable men and the charitable women, the sacrificing men and the sacrificing women." It always puts the believers of rank together.

If we are going to build a society that the world can admire, we cannot be guilty of oppression or suppression or racism or sexism or materialism, or any kind of "ism." We must grow to see with the Eyes of God. We must grow to emote with the Heart of God. We must become acquainted with His Way of thinking and doing. This is not asked of us. This is demanded of us in this serious hour in which we live.

## Fostering the development of women

I am particularly proud to foster the development of our women in the spiritual areas where women in the traditional respect have not had a role, particularly in Islam. I am not trying to fly in the face of the Islamic world and say to my dear and beloved Brothers and Sisters of faith to say that they do not know what they are saying or doing, far be that from me as a baby in Islam. However, it is written in the scriptures [Psalm 8:2] that out of the mouth of babes will come wisdom. I respectfully urge the people of religion all over the world to rethink their views with respect to womanhood. If we are going to build a society where God is lifted, then we must respect what Allah (God) has put in the female. We must honor it. We must provide an atmosphere where what Allah (God) has deposited in women can be nurtured, developed, and expressed.

Our leader and teacher, the Honorable Elijah Muhammad wanted women to have a base in the home. He said that the home was their base but their place even. I understand after looking deeply into the words of the Honorable Elijah Muhammad. Women in this world are not utilized for the purpose of which Allah (God) intended. In this world, women are used as playthings, the pleasure baskets of men and boys only to be used and discarded, only to be made pregnant and left alone with your offspring to fend for yourselves.

Since the world is so disrespectful of women, and since women represent that power from God that nurtures and evolves and shapes the destiny of the nation, then a foolish man will be a man who will not put protection around his woman. A Wise Man will protect his woman. "Are you saying that women cannot protect themselves?" In the nature of things, God has always made man the protector of the woman, though some women today are so strong and aggressive, they have reversed the role and have become the protectors of the men.

We should be protectors of each other. The Qur'an says [Surah 2:187] that the man is as an apparel for the woman and the woman is as an apparel for the man. Apparel is clothing and clothing is given to protect you from natural elements. God gives man a woman to protect him from the natural inclination of his urges and likewise the female. But it extends beyond the urges, that we should be protectors of one another.

Because of the way the male's biology and physiology is constructed, he is, by his strength, to be the protector. His home should be the secure place of that man. The woman is the treasure of the nation. He does not expose his treasure to thieves and robbers who would come in and steal. He is wise if he puts his wife and daughters in his home where he, as the protector and defender of the virtue of his wife, can protect the sanity and sanctity of his family by keeping them in an environment that he controls.

When we spread our control from our home into the community, and we control the workplace, we control the politics, we control every facet of the life of that nation, if the same righteousness that is seen in the home can be seen in the government, then our women can come out of the home and go forward in a protected environment in government, law, medicine, and wherever her gifts may be, but she must be protected. She must be defended from the filth of an environment that if it corrupts her, it corrupts our future. We are not in control of the society—its education, politics, or anything of this world. We may have some measure of control over our homes, so we want our wives and daughters in a place where we can defend their righteousness and virtue. This has been so misread. "Keep the woman pregnant. Keep her in the house. You can keep her barefoot and you will have a happy home." That is awful ignorance. It is very oppressive and suppressive of what Allah (God) has created in the female for the betterment of herself, her family, and her nation.

Under the light of the guidance of the Honorable Elijah Muhammad, he instilled in us as men the spirit to move out from our homes and control our environment. Wherever we can move and control the environment, we bring our women into that environment to help us with management, operations, and planning. The man must move out as the pioneer. He must be the one to cut down the underbrush and shoulder the weapon and kill the beasts and the savages if he can't civilize them. And then set up an outpost and then bring his woman and say you are secure here. Now, let's go and plan for the compound or plan for the education or plan for the welfare of our family.

Men have misused the thought of women being in their homes. So, women now rebel against the home. Men want to keep you there as a means of suppressing you because they are not reaching out to control anything that might advance you in the society. That is a form of oppression. Women, in order to reject oppression, they reject homelife. They reject cooking as though that is some terrible thing. They reject sewing. They reject being a good mother. They reject being a good wife and taking care of a man. They don't understand that if there is no happiness in the home, there can be no happiness in the society. Happiness as well as peace must start in the home. There can be no peace in the home unless there is understanding between the male and the female, and not burdening each other with attacks on one another when we should be working together for the common good of the whole.

## Growing into the Mind of God

Today, I want to share a basic understanding of the working of the Mind of Allah (God) and why it is necessary that we grow into His Mind. Women are important if we are to grow into the Mind of God. We can never keep women out of the Houses of God. We can never keep women away from the Words of God. If the nation is fashioned by a woman, then what fashions the woman? The woman must be fashioned by the only perfect thing that can nurture and shape both woman and man—the Word of Almighty God Allah.

If our women are fashioned, shaped, nurtured, evolved and developed by the Word of Allah (God), then our women will evolve and develop our children according to the plan of Allah (God). To baptize our minds in the Words of God is to begin to think after His Word. To think after the Word of God is to act after the Mind of God. Then, you can bring your children into His Mind, and they will grow even more deeply into the reality of His thinking than their parents. This is how society progresses, ever spiraling upward, but the base of that society is a woman whose mind is baptized in the Words of God.

Prophet Muhammad (PBUH) said heaven lies at the feet of mother. Why at her feet? At her feet means obedience or submission to her. If heaven lies at her feet, then her head must be in the right place in order for heaven to be at her feet. Her head must be in the Word of Allah (God), in obedience to Allah (God) in order for heaven to be at her feet. Because if heaven can be at her feet, hell can also be there too.

What does this have to do with 1987 and life as we know it? Dear beloved Brothers and Sisters, as we struggle through this life, there are many trials and tribulations that each one of us must go through in order to reap the fullness of life. Life cannot bring us her treasures without trial, nor will you know the value of yourself without trial. You will not know the beauty of God without trial, tribulation, and great pain and suffering.

Someone asked me is pain necessary for growth. I said yes. There can be no growth without pain. There's a difference between pain inflicted in the natural process of our evolution toward God and pain inflicted by a wicked person who intends to torture us by pain to break our will or make us respond to the pain in such a way that we do their bidding. We're not talking about torture. Torture is not pain. Torture is excruciating pain beyond the limit of one's capacity to endure. Once you get beyond the limit of our capacity to endure, that kind of pain is excruciating. The longer it continues, it becomes torture. The Qur'an teaches us [Surah 2:191] that "persecution is worse than slaughter." That kind of torture on a human being is worse than death. God has ordained pain but each of us has a threshold beyond which pain cannot be endured without breaking the person, the will, the spirit, and even the mind.

If a woman is made by Allah (God) to bear the excruciating pain of birth, which has its only equal in the pain of death, then you are made to bear both the pains of life and the pain of death and hold on. Torture is very, very different from that.

## Attitude through suffering

Pain is necessary. Each one of us in order to come to where we are now, has had to go through some kind of pain, some kind of trial, some kind of tribulation. Reflect for a moment with me on your own self, nobody else, and your trials, tribulations and pain, and your attitude as you go through these things. All praise is due to Allah. There are many different attitudes that we can take when we suffer. "Why me? As much as I pray. As hard as I work. Why me? I see so and so over there, they aren't any good. They don't pray. I don't see them do nothing for God. Why didn't He take their daughter, not mine. Why didn't He kill her husband, not mine?" Attitude.

"I'm going to school and the teacher is making it hard for me." Attitude. How do you handle it? What's my attitude? "I'll just quit. I'll walk out on this." Fine. You're not hurting the teacher. Who are you hurting? The government is persecuting us because we want to be Muslims. How do you handle it? What is your attitude towards your persecutors and tormentors? Every one of us has gone through something where we question the Wisdom of God. "If you're God, God, why do Black people suffer like this?" That's a good question. "If you're God, God, why did you allow this war between Iran and Iraq and so many children being slaughtered? If you're God, God, and nothing happens but by Your permission, why would you permit such horror to take place on the earth?" It's not wrong to question, but it is the attitude that we take in our questioning.

If we say, "I don't want to believe in you no more." Hey, it's alright. He was God before you came into the world. He'll be God when you leave. Your belief does not help Him. He's not sitting in heaven waiting on you to believe. He's not necessarily worried that you don't believe. Your belief in Him helps you. Doesn't do anything for Him. You can't add to Him by your belief, nor can you detract from Him by your disbelief. You can add to yourself, or you can take away from yourself. That's for you and for me. Attitude through suffering. Allah (God) does not think like you think and I think. Allah (God) and His Ways are not your ways nor my ways. His timeframe is not your timeframe or my timeframe. God does things for an overall purpose that leads ultimately to the greatest good for all of us. "I don't believe that." I'm going to prove it.

Your suffering, whether you know it or not, even if it's brought about by your own misdeeds or my misdeeds, the suffering is not commensurate with the deed. Even in the suffering, God is merciful when He applies the weight of consequence so that you are not destroyed for your evil. You are punished with a slight portion of the consequence, so that you may reflect and turn from the course that you are on and say, "I surrender. I submit to the Will of God."

**The perfection of humanity**

Everything about Allah (God) and the Way He works with His creatures revolves around four major attributes. Today, I want to talk to you about them, give you some parables from the Qur'an and my understanding of those parables, and then we can go home. If we say all our prayers, every Muslim says the *Al-Fatihah* or "The Opening" of the Qur'an a minimum of 32 times a day. The 32nd Surah of the Qur'an is called "The Adoration." Water freezes at 32 [degrees]. Anything below 32 is frozen. Anything above 32 starts thawing out. There's a lot of wisdom in that. The Remembrance of God. The four major Attributes of God are the foundation of all His Attributes, of which they are 99. Allah (God) makes us recite these four attributes 32 times a day.

What are these attributes? The first verse of the Qur'an begins with *Alhamdulillah,* "Praise belongs to God," followed by the Attributes – Who is the Lord, Nourisher, Sustainer, Evolver of all the worlds, making them attain stage after stage until they reach their eventual perfection. What is God's ultimate aim for His creatures? Perfection. He will perfect the sun. He will perfect the moon, the stars, and the earth. He will perfect man. He will perfect His Light. His ultimate aim is perfection. Allah (God) is in charge of the process by which we reach perfection. Keep that in mind.

Then, we are made to say the two chief Attributes of Allah (God) – *Al Rahman, Al Rahim,* The Beneficent, The Merciful. Out of His Love, He creates everything that we need to go exactly where He desires us to go. There is nothing that you need to become a perfected human being that is not already here in existence. It was here for you before you were born. That is a Beneficent Creator and a Merciful Creator.

He did not ask you to pay Him. It is an underserved kindness. He reigns water on [Mikhail] Gorbachev, and He drops water on [Ronald] Reagan. Think about that. He puts the sunlight on the wicked as well as the just. It's an undeserved kindness. His principal attributes are beneficence and mercy.

The Message of God should never be delivered out of the emotion of hatred. The Message of God cannot be delivered out of an emotion of hostility. The Message of God must be delivered out of the spirit of the Giver of that message Who is The Beneficent and

The Merciful, whose aim is the perfection of humanity. You think about what I am saying and argue with it if you will.

## A righteous mentality

The Qur'an says to those who teach the faith [Surah 16:125]: "Call to the way of your Lord with wisdom and goodly exhortation and argue with them in the best manner." You don't call people to God for vain purposes, for them to see how smart you are, how great you are how intelligent you are how this you are. That's the wrong motive. Don't call the people to God with hostility. Don't call the people to God with vengeance only as the motivation for preaching the Word of God. Even though vengeance is in His attributes, mercy encompasses all things. It takes precedence over vengeance. If you preach the Word of God with a vengeful spirit, then you are absolutely in disharmony with the nature of the God that you represent, out of harmony with the spirit of the God that you represent—that is, if you represent the God of righteousness.

No God ever sent a prophet to preach, even to the wicked, out of hostility. When Moses went to Pharaoh, he never said to him, "Pharoah, your time has come, you wicked dog. God is going to destroy you. There are 10 plagues He told me to run it down to you, baby." Excuse me if I sound a little savage. In the Qur'an, Allah (God) tells Moses to speak "a gentle word" to Pharoah that perhaps he may mind [Surah 20:44]. The objective of God is always to change your mind and change the road that you're traveling on. His Hope is that you will accept His Mercy in warning that He will not have to use His Power to bring you to total ruin and destruction. He's slow to anger and quick to forgive.

He's Beneficent. He's Merciful. He is the Master of the Law of Requital. He's not a judge who has to go by the law. Any judge who is downtown, some of them we meet a lot, must judge according to the law. "I'm very sorry, the law says such and such and you were guilty. Therefore, you must…" A Master of the law can forgive sins altogether without any penalty or He can bring His Wrath down as

He pleases on whom He pleases when He pleases. All are guilty. The Qur'an says if Allah (God) punishes man for his sins, not one soul would be left alive on the earth [Surah 16:61]. All of us are in need of His Mercy not His punishment. We hope for His Mercy, and we fear His Chastisement. That's a righteous mentality.

**Our means of subsistence**

Let's look at our problems. You don't have enough money. That's a problem. That's a real problem. That's a heavy problem. I'm glad I mentioned that one first. The rent is due. The lights are going to be cut off. I don't want to steal. I have this gun in my coat pocket and there's an unsuspecting lady out there who just got paid. I can't get evicted. What am I going to do?

The weak side of self says, "Go get the money and deal with the moral question later." The strong side of self says, "I am Allah. Trust in me. I have your wealth in My hand. I straighten the means of subsistence for whom I please and I amplify it for whom I please. Would you not like to come into My Favor? Trust me. The birds are eating. The buzzards eat. Even the skunk has something to eat. Baboons and orangutans eat. Fish in the sea eat. You are My servant. Do you think I want you to starve? O ye of little faith."

I'm trying to teach you a lesson through your own poor condition. Poverty is a condition made by circumstances here (*points to his head*), but the universe is a giant breast of God. It cannot withhold its blessings from you if you know how to draw on that breast and believe that God did not bring you into the earth to cause you to suffer. He brought you here to give His Favor to you.

As a baby, you can draw from the breast of your mother, not knowing whether there's milk there. By nature, you know how to suck on the breasts, and you believe that there's something there for you. So, you keep on pulling until you get something. Paul said [Hebrews 11:1], "Faith is the substance of things hoped for, the evidence of things not seen." The baby doesn't know anything about substance in the breast, but the baby has a faith that something is

17

here. So, it keeps on pulling and that pulling was rewarded with some nourishment. The universe is a giant mammary gland of God. It cannot withhold its blessing from you if you approach it properly. It is created by God to be subservient to man, so says the Holy Qur'an [Surah 22:18]. If you're poor, it's because you've approached it poorly. If God straightens the means by which you subsist, that doesn't mean cutting it out altogether. It means drawing it up, so you get a little pain and pinch. When you look at your money, it's a pinch. The Qur'an says [Surahs 59:9, 64:16] that men should strive to be saved from the greediness of his own soul. When your money is pinched, you don't want to give anything in charity. Allah (God) says in the Qur'an [Surah 2:177] that the true and righteous person is one who knows that the poor and the destitute have a right to some of his wealth.

If God straightens your means of subsistence, how do you handle it? What is your attitude? "I'm going to steal. I'm going to cheat." No! "My God is not a crook. He doesn't want me to be that." In fact, stealing is so cheapening to the character of the human being that, when you realize what stealing is, you should never even entertain the thought.

The Qur'anic punishment for stealing is cutting off the hands. On the spiritual or metaphysical plane, whenever you steal, you are cutting off the Hand of God from aiding you. You are cutting off your ability to retrieve from the universe what you are justly due. God does not make thieves. Any one of you who steals, you need to cut it out instantly because you are discrediting yourself. You are not allowing God to use His power through you to enrich you out of His Grace. Crookedness is not tolerated by God.

God amplifies the means of subsistence for some of us. The pimp and drug addict look like they have a wad of money. You are righteous and don't have any money. "God, why you do that? Why do you lay that on the pimp? How can the pimp ride a big car and I'm here on the bus? God seems so unjust." Allah (God) says in the Qur'an He gives men that for which they strive [Surah 42:20]. If this world is what you strive for, He'll give it to you. The life of the Hereafter is not a spook life; it's a life lived on a much higher plane than this life. Allah (God) said I'll give those who want the life of the Hereafter that life. If you are wise, you all will want that kind of life.

Allah (God) says [Surah 89:15-16] to you I'm trying you by what I offer you both in straightening your means or amplifying it. It is a trial to all of you. The man who has much, how will you act? Will you give away some of your substance to the poor? Will you remember the Creator Who made it possible for you to become rich? Or will you deny Him and walk around like the wicked in arrogance and pride, thinking that you deserve this? This is not what you deserve. This is the undeserved grace and kindness of God.

We only have one more minute left in this broadcast. Those of you in the listening audience, I wish you were here. If the broadcast cuts off, just remember that the Light will never cut off from you if you don't cut off from it.

## Acquiring the heart of humility

Some of you have lost a loved one. Some of you get into situations and, with the way you think, you cannot come up with a real logical explanation for what God does. God does not function from your logic. You must first understand how finite we are. You just got here and if you're not careful you are going to leave very soon. Even if you are careful, we're going to leave soon. How could our finite lives grapple with the mysteries unless God Himself helps us to see beyond when we came in and when we go out.

Why did God take my sister-in-law who died last week, leaving six children? Why did God take Moses? Why did God take Jesus? Why did God take Muhammad or Abraham and the prophets? Why interfere with such beautiful life and bring death here? What is Your purpose, God? You know we love these people. Why do you take them and then they put such a burden on our heart of grief and sorrow? Why in the scheme of things Allah will you allow Iran and Iraq to continue to fight? They are Muslims and they're slaughtering

19

each other. Why Beirut and Lebanon destroyed? What is going on Allah? What do you have in mind? "It's horrible." From what vantage point? The vantage point of your logic. It's your logic. How did you grow to think like you think? What is the base of the process by which you arrive at conclusions?

It is a mathematics that could be erroneous. Even if it is perfect, it is limited to your scope. You must understand that your scope of knowledge is very limited. If I ask you to see what's going on in the room—Brother in the front, see what's going on in the room. You can't look at me and see what's going on in the room. You must turn and look and check and you still may not see everything because there's people you can't see. All you can testify to is the range of your vision. What is the range of your vision? It is limited according to the light.

If we turn the lights out, you may see nothing. "I can't tell what's going on." It is not your eyes that must calculate the incalculable. Therefore, God says to us in the Bible and Qur'an, judgment is Allah's (God's). To the Muslims who say we who follow the Honorable Elijah Muhammad are not true Muslims, when did you become the judge? "I judge by the Qur'an." Who said you understand it? "The words are plain." Who said so? Allah (God) said [Surah 3:7] there are words in the Qur'an that are plain but there are words that are for the learned and the scholar. Are you they and how dare you arrogate scholarship to yourself? What have you done with your scholarship that bears witness that you are a scholar? Nothing. Confuse the people and upset the world and made it as though the prophets have never even existed.

Please, please, please, we must acquire the heart of humility and recognize that Allah (God) alone is worthy to judge. We can with the Qur'an make judgments, but we must leave room in our judgment for fallacious thinking. We must leave room in our judgment for the probability of being incorrect. Our knowledge is not absolute. God tells you in your prayer to say, "I have been greatly unjust to myself." Then, if you are unjust to yourself, you must be unjust to others. So how can you who are unjust be a true judge of justice unless Allah (God) permits it.

## Male and female, evolving to reflect God

I'm coming to a very important point. I hope it's important to you. Muslims believe that Muhammad ibn Abdullah of Arabia is the Seal of the Prophets of God. If Muhammad is the Seal of the Prophets, that means no more prophets are coming into the world. This book Qur'an is the final revelation from Allah (God) to humanity. No more prophets. No more books. This is it. Right? Wrong. Right? Right. Where is it right and where is it wrong?

I'm not being smart or funny, but teaching should never be a chore and learning should never be a chore. It must be a wonderful experience, for both of us because I am not only imparting but I am learning, too.

Prophet Muhammad did bring the final revelation. No question. Prophet Muhammad is the end of the prophets, the last prophet. No question. But what is your condition and what is the condition of the world? Prophets come to explain. Do you need some explanation? Everyone in the world needs someone to explain something to us because we're all confused. Religion is confused. Politics is confused. Education is confused. You are confused. Do you need a teacher?

Prophets are raised to explain. If he explained it and he's the last one, then we don't need any more interpretation. We don't need any more explanation. We can move and execute on the Will of God because we know it now.

Prophets come to reform. Is that what they do? If he's the last one, shouldn't we be reformed? We should be on the right track, making it unnecessary for a prophet ever to come again. I'm sorry about this but Saudi Arabia needs reform. Mecca needs reform. Iran, Iraq, Egypt need reform. The Christian world needs reform. Jews and Buddhists need reform. In fact, the whole world needs reform. How could the last prophet have been?

Prophets come to warn and guide. Do we need warning? Do we need guidance? What will we use? If Muhammad (PBUH) is the end of the prophets, then we should be in a better condition. Something needs to be understood. What is it that needs to be understood? Brothers and Sisters, this is so beautiful.

Christians will argue vehemently, "Muhammad is great, but Jesus Christ is the man." How are you going to contend with Christians? Many Christians in here today, you don't know anything about Muhammad. Your Bible tells you about Jesus.

I love him. Muslims, the Qur'an teaches us about Allah but makes Muhammad the door to Allah. When you are among Muslims, they say, *Ashadu an la ilaha illa illa-ilah, wa ashadu anna muhammadan rasul ullah,* "I bear witness that there's no God but Allah and I bear witness that Muhammad is the Messenger of God." What about the Christian? Christians say that I bear witness that God is God and that Jesus is God in man.

Muslims say, "*Astagfirullah!* What are you saying Christians?!" *A virgin conceived.* "Yes, go on." *It was a child of a Holy Ghost. A baby was born, and it grew up and became God.* Muslims say, "*Astagfirullah! Qul huwa l-lāhu 'ahad(un). Allāhu ṣ-ṣamad(u). Lam yalid walam yūlad; Walam yaku n-lahū kufu'an ahad(un):* "Say He, Allah, is One. Allah is He of Whom nothing is independent but upon Whom we all depend. He begets not nor is He begotten, and there is none like Him" [Surah 112:1-4]. The Qur'an says [Surah 4:171], "And say not, Three. Desist, it is better for you. Allah is only one God." There's an argument between Muslims and Christians. How do you resolve it? How do you reconcile it? Let me help you by the Help of Allah (God).

Muslims are not wrong in what they say, but the Christians have truth on their side too. "What? Is a Muslim going to argue the point of a Christian?" I cannot argue the point of labels. We can only argue the point of truth. This Qur'an says [Surah 17:70] that man— meaning male and female—are born into the world with a capacity to master what God has created. This Qur'an calls man God's "khalifah"—His successor, vicegerent [Surah 6:165]. We have the capacity to dominate and master this realm. We can master the forces of nature by Allah's (God's) Permission. We are born. We come from a woman. We were begotten.

Even though we were begotten, we can evolve by Allah's (God's) Permission to perfection where we reflect Allah (God) perfectly in this realm. We can master the laws that govern creation. We have that capacity. Then, we have the capacity to evolve to reflect God in a man. Allah (God) says to us, "I give you permission to wear My attributes." Why would He do such a thing? Is He setting up gods beside Himself? He alone is Muhammad, worthy of praise, but He can give "Muhammad" to you. He alone is Alim, The Best Knower, but He shares His knowledge with you and says you can call yourself "Alim." He alone is Hakeem, Aziz, and Jabbar, but He allows you to wear these names because you have the essence that is in Him. He has given it to you. If you allow God to evolve you to perfection, He can make you a perfect reflection of Himself, not that you are Him. There is none like Allah (God), but He said, I can make you reflect Me.

## Our conversation with God

Let's get to this problem of messengership and prophethood. Here's how the Christians view it, the Muslims view it, and how we can make these two views reconcile. Muhammad is the Last Prophet of God. Muhammad brings the Qur'an. There is not another revelation that came into the world since this Qur'an. It is a perfect and pure book. This book is so right and exact it is the most marvelous act of God as He intervenes in the affairs of men to give us His thinking and His mind. He doesn't say to Muhammad, "Think it through." He says, when they say this to you, Muhammad, you say.

Brother [Muammar] Qadhafi in Libya said that was to Muhammad and therefore we should take out the "Say." I said to Brother Qadhafi, no dear brother, leave the "say" in because God is still saying, though He is not saying to Muhammad of Arabia. He saying to you who would have a conversation with Him. When you read the Qur'an, you're having a conversation with God Himself. If you have a conversation with God, how can you come away stupid? If you converse with God every day, how can you come away an imbecile? If you allow God to speak to you daily and nightly until His Words permeate your mind, then will you think like you or will you think like Him?

Bear with me. That's why it's good for me to go away and stay a couple of weeks. This builds up in me, and, to tell you the truth, maybe you all can't take me every week. Maybe I can't take myself every week (smile). It's wise to let you feed on something and then go away and let me feed too. What we're saying is not revolutionary but, by the Grace of the Allah (God), it is inspiring I believe to know why Christians and Muslims should be together.

Jesus said, "My thoughts are not your thoughts, neither your ways my ways"; Mine are from above while yours is from beneath [Isaiah 55:8-9]. Paul says [Philippians 2:5], "Let this mind be in you, which was also in Christ Jesus." Jesus said not my will but Your Will [Luke 22:42], and whatever I hear in my ear from my Father that I speak [Matthew 10:27]. When God speaks to Jesus, Jesus speaks to the people.

Jesus and Muhammad must be closely related because whatever God said to Muhammad, Muhammad spoke it to the people. The Bible gives us what Jesus did but very little of what Jesus said. This (holding up the Qur'an) is the book of what Jesus said. The Bible is the book of what Jesus did. When you put them together, you have the word and the action, the blood and the bread of the ability to commune with God.

Read your Bible. Jesus was by the Sea of Galilee, and he said blessed are ye who mourn [Matthew 5:4], blessed are the pure in heart [Matthew 5:8], and also a few parables. Matthew says it from his view. Mark says it from his view. Luke says it from his view. John says it from his view. The words of Jesus in some of Bibles are written in red. If you extract all the red text of what Jesus said, you will have just a little bit of text.

Here's a book (holding up the Qur'an) with the Words of God revealed to a man. When acted upon, these words will make it unnecessary for a prophet to ever have to come again. It is not Muhammad who closes the door on prophets. It is you. He's the Seal; he brought the stuff to seal it with, but you haven't used the sealer yet. Here's a man who tells you, here's polyurethane, put it on the wall and it will seal the wall. The wall is porous. The sealer is in the corner. Here's the brush. Water is getting into the bricks. "Muhammad is the Seal. Muhammad is the Seal. Muhammad is the Seal." Yes, he's the Seal, but will you get up and use the sealer? How are you going to tell me he is the Seal, but you have never opened the book. You won't read the book. You won't study the book. You won't live the book. Then you need a reformer today because Muhammad is dead and gone, and the world is confused.

Don't tell me Jesus is the answer, Jesus is the way. When are you going to apply the answer? When are you going to walk in the way? Preachers say, Jesus said, "I am the door [John 10:9]. I am the true vine John 15:1]." *Go ahead, reverend, preach it, preach it, preach it!* Christians say Jesus is the door, but when did you enter? If you entered, why are you in the shape you are in? How could you be a n---- and have entered through the door? I don't understand it. N----s do not go through the door. Righteous people went in there. You don't go through the door a homosexual. If you entered the door, on the other side of the door you are a new person. Why are you not made new?

Why do we need reformation? We have not adopted the seal. We have not used this. "O Allah, Your ways are not ours and Your thoughts are not ours. Because we refused to think like You think and walk in Your ways, our judgment, like our vision, is so limited. Therefore, we make such mistakes. Our logic is confusion."

## Patience in the absence of comprehensive knowledge

In Surah 18 of the Qur'an entitled "The Cave," Moses is traveling in search of knowledge. He meets a Wise Man, and he

25

wants to walk with the Wise Man. It didn't say a wise spirit, it said a Wise Man because God deals with men and women through men and women. He doesn't send spooks. The Qur'an says had you been an angel, He would have sent you an angel [Surah 17:95]. You are a man and a woman, so He sends you a man and a woman, mainly man, to deal with you.

Moses tells the Wise Man that he wants to follow him. The Wise Man lays down some preconditions. Moses said, "May I follow you that you may teach me of the good that you have been taught." The Qur'an says of this great and mighty master who would come in the end of the world [Surah 53:5-6], "One Mighty in Power has taught him, The Lord of Strength, so he attained to perfection."

We don't reach perfection without a teacher. One mighty in power taught the teacher. Moses said, can I follow you that I can learn the good that you have been taught. The Wise Man said thou canst not have patience with me." Wait a minute. The Qur'an says Allah (God) created us impatient but to follow a Wise Man, patience is demanded of us. Patience is the ability to endure long suffering to reap the reward of the fulfillment of your desire.

"If it had been a short journey and a near gain, they all would have gone forth." But this kind of word is not for those who are looking for a short journey and a little cheap goal. The goal is to attain God Himself and that's a lifelong journey. One must be patient and long-suffering, so Jesus said [Ecclesiastes 9:11], "The race is not to the swift but to the one who can endure to the end."

The Wise Man told Moses, "You can't have patience with me." He knew him. Moses said, "If Allah please, you will find me patient, nor shall I disobey you in anything." This is a man talking to another man who was taught. The Honorable Elijah Muhammad said this is not a prophet. Prophets don't follow Allah (God) like that.

Moses was a prophet of God, but the word "Moses" is used to hide the reality that this is talking about how people will follow the man that God gives them, like Moses who led a people out of the bondage of their condition. You follow men of wisdom with doubt and suspicion. The Wise Man asked, "How can you have patience in that whereof you have not a comprehensive knowledge?" He was saying your vision is so limited, how can you have patience if you don't know the beginning or the end of where you are going? How can you be patient with me?

Moses never came back with the right answer. He said, "If Allah please, you will find me patient." That's not the answer. When he was asked, "*How* can you have patience in that whereof you don't have a comprehensive knowledge, he should have said, "My sight is limited but I believe. I have faith that you will guide me right. Therefore, I will walk in the light of faith. Because I don't have a comprehensive knowledge, faith will lead me until the comprehensive knowledge is in sight." But the man didn't give the right answer. His answer showed that he was going to stumble and fall. He said, "If Allah please." That sounds good. "You will find me patient." Look at how bold he is: "I will not disobey you in anything." This man was really something.

Then the Wise Man said, "If you will follow me, question me not about anything until I myself speak to you about it." Good God Almighty! That's a heavy thing. If you have a husband, he can't tell you, "Don't question me about anything until I myself speak to you about it." You tell him, "Wait a minute, honey! Where were you last night? You told me you were going to be at the barbershop. I went by there at the time you said you were going to be there but you weren't there. Now, where were you?" *I told you don't speak to me about anything until I speak to you.* You would be so distrustful of that man. That's a heavy trial for someone to tell you don't speak to them about something unless they speak to you about it.

Here's the journey. They set out on a journey, and they embarked on a boat. The Wise Man made a hole in the boat. They were just getting started and the Wise Man puts a hole in the boat. Moses said, "Hey!" Excuse me, that's not in the translation (smile). Moses said, "Have you made a hole in it to drown its occupants? I'm in the boat with you and you put a hole in the boat?!" Moses is judging right away. He said, "You have surely done a grievous thing." He jumped right on him, judgmental, "You did a grievous thing." Grievous, how? "It's grieving the hell out of me. I'm suffering seeing water come in the boat. I can't swim." The Wise Man said, "Did I not say that you could not have patience with me." Moses said, "Blame me not for what I forgot."

He's like [President Ronald] Reagan, can't remember. Moses said, for God's sake, don't be hard on me for what I did. Reagan talking about it was a mistake. You ought to stop that, Reagan. That's not a mistake. A mistake is an unintentional departure from what is correct. He purposely knew what he was doing. He made an error. He wants to minimize it. "It's a little mistake. What do you do? You take your lumps, and you move on." Who said God wants you to move on after you take your lumps?

Moses and the Wise Man patched it up. We're on the journey now. They went on until when they met a boy. The Wise Man slew the boy. Moses said, "Have you slain an innocent person not guilty of slaying another? You have indeed done a horrible thing." He's getting worse in his language. The more the journey continues, he gets unbearable. He tells the Wise Man that he did a horrible thing but, at first, he told him, I want to follow you so that I can benefit from what you were taught. Then he told the man that he did a grievous thing when he put a hole in the boat, and now he did a horrible thing when he killed the woman's child.

The Wise Man said, "Did I not say to you that you could not have patience with me?" Moses said, "If I ask you about anything after this, don't keep company with me anymore and you will indeed then have found an excuse in my case."—an excuse to walk away from me because I excused you by my ignorant performance. They patched it up. The Qur'an says, "So they went on until they came to the people of a town and they asked its people for food but the people refused to entertain them as guests."

Think about it. You're hungry and come into a town and say, "I'm traveling. Can I get something to eat please?" *No, away with you.*

When they were refused food, they found a wall on the point of falling near the house. The Wise Man put the wall into a right state. Here's some people who just refused to give him food, but he sees a broken-down wall near their house. And he patches it up. Moses is real hot now and jumps on him.

Moses said, "If you had wished…" I can hear him, especially if he was a Negro. He said, "Maaaan, is you crazy? Look how hungry we are. We went to the people. They had fish. I could smell the fish and we asked them for food. They didn't give us none. We could have said to them, I will build the wall if you give me some food. But no, you fixed the bad wall, and I am hungry." The Wise Man said, "Look Jack!" This is a modern translation of this Qur'an (smile). He said, "Look Jack, this is the parting between me and thee. But before I split—I mean, before I go, I will inform you of the significance of that which you could not have patience with me. I'm going to teach you, but we have to part company."

Remember the points: The Wise Man said, "How can you have patience with me if you don't have a comprehensive knowledge." But the man didn't even have faith in the wise man he was following. So, if he didn't have comprehensive knowledge and didn't have faith, they would have to part company.

He said, as for the boat—it belonged to poor people working on the river. I damaged the boat purposely because there was a wicked king who was seizing boats by force. I didn't want these poor people to lose their boat. So, I damaged the boat. I put a hole in it. A hole is not damage. It will sink the boat but when the wicked king passes over, they can retrieve the boat, plug up the hole, and sail again. Can you dig it? Excuse me for being so hip today.

As for the boy I slew—his parents were believers. We feared lest he should involve them in wrongdoing and disbelief so we intended that their Lord might give them in his place one better in purity and nearer to mercy. So, we took away from that righteous couple an offspring that might have led them into evil and gave them a better child in its place. And as for the wall—it belonged to two orphan boys in the city. There was beneath it a treasure belonging to them and their father had been a righteous man so thy Lord intended that they should obtain their maturity and get their treasure, a mercy from thy Lord. I did not do it of my own accord. This is the significance of that with which you could not have patience."

Since we don't have a comprehensive knowledge of what God's plan is, even for ourselves, as He evolves us toward perfection, when a misfortune comes into your life, don't throw up your hands as though a wicked thing has taken place, even though evil is written on the face of what you suffer.

Face it with this mind: Allah (God) is The Beneficent. He is The Merciful. He doesn't intend suffering for me except for my advancement. He is my *Raab*—my Lord, my nurturer, my nourisher into perfection and He creates and masters the circumstances that will evolve me toward Him. So, if an evil afflicts me, should I curse Him? I say, all praise is due to Allah. He is my patron. This that I am going through, Allah (God) will help me to go through it because it's only a part of my journey toward Him. The Beneficent, The Merciful. He is master of this. He could afflict me with it entirely or He could remove some of it. He chooses to allow me to suffer some pain. In His Name, I'll go through it because I know that in the end His Will is good for us all.

## Closing the door on prophethood

Beloved, to talk like that is easy but to live like that is the test. I respectfully submit to you that the world is suffering not because of some evil of God but the world is suffering because of the disobedience of man and woman and our rejection of the right guidance given by the prophets of God. Allah (God) is allowing humanity to taste a part of what we have done so that perhaps we may return.

[Ayatollah] Khomeini in Iran, I believe, is a righteous-intended man but he came on the heels of the Shah who may also have been right intended but he felt that Islam could not bring Iran into the modern world. So, the Shah succumbed to the power of the West, their technology, and their way of civilization. They corrupted the way of Islam because the ruler himself did not have any faith in Islam. Islam is not a religion for yesterday. It is for all time. The Qur'an is a modern book, but we must come to it with a modern technology to mine the rich resources out of the Qur'an to guide us every day of our lives. So, we judge. The Shah is no good, Khomeini is good. Or Khomeini is no good, the Shah is good. No! Allah (God) is good. Both are serving a purpose.

The Honorable Elijah Muhammad built this community. He made us something from nothing, Brothers and Sisters, by the Power of Allah (God). He departed from us, and his son Imam Warithudeen took the community another way. We who loved the Honorable Elijah Muhammad were all in pain. What happened? "All that we built is gone," we cried. We said Wallace is good, his father is bad, or we said the father is good and Wallace is bad. I say neither. Allah (God) is good. Allah (God) is The Greatest. Nothing happened but by the Permission of Allah (God). If He permitted it *(recording skips)*, we suffered whatever we suffered. Allah (God) is involved in it all.

We are in our little judgmental bags. This is a hypocrite. This is a believer. This is a true Muslim. I'm the true believer. I'm the true follower. Farrakhan's a hypocrite. No, I'm the believer, you're the hypocrite. I'm judging and you're in trouble. All of you are a bunch of d---n fools. Why don't you shut up and let Allah (God) have His way. He's the Master of it all. Shut up. You're suffering? So, what. You are not the first people who suffered, and you won't be the last. God's end is good for every one of us if we take and go through it with steadfastness.

We were in a boat with a Wise Man. The boat is the Nation. It's like the ark. A hole was put in the boat and the Nation began to sink. I could hear, "What's wrong with you, putting a hole in the boat I'm in?" The two parents who had a child who would maybe lead the parents back into disbelief—maybe we, as followers of Islam, were not strong. Maybe if we grew up the way we were growing up, we might have been a curse on our own nation. So, the first children had to be nullified. God killed the first born of Pharaoh so that the second born wouldn't take after the first born. Why does Allah (God) say in the Qur'an that He'll raise a new generation. There will be a second group and they will not be like the first group. He'll bring another group in your place, the Qur'an says [Surah 5:54].

We who followed the Honorable Elijah Muhammad followed him with doubt and suspicion, just like that man followed the Wise Man. We didn't know what the Honorable Elijah Muhammad was doing. We couldn't see. We didn't have a comprehensive knowledge, but he was taught by a Wise God. He knew the beginning and the end of this thing. He saw it all. He saw his son coming and he knew what his son was going to do, and he prepared for it. In the end, what his son did was going to serve the Nation even though his heart may not have been pure or right. Leave that to God to judge. The result will be beneficial to us all.

I implore you to let us try to grow into the Mind of God. It's difficult. I have a problem like you trying to grow into Allah's (God's) Way of looking at things so that we don't get so judgmental and hung up and fall out bitter and hateful. It's not necessary. You can't stop what God has willed. His Will is going to prevail. It's going to be established. So do the best you can.

The more you think in the manner that God would be pleased, then you yourself become the Seal of the Prophets. Not that you are the Muhammad, but you use the sealer, and you make it unnecessary for a prophet ever to come again. Once you are in the Mind and Spirit of God, you are a witness not of a God to come or a God Who was. You are a witness that God is present in your very life. Therefore, by that state of being, you have closed the door on prophethood. All praise is due to Allah. Thank you for listening. I greet you in peace. *As-Salaam Alaikum!*

.

# 3 THE LIBERATION OF WOMEN IN RELIGION

In The Name of Allah, The Beneficent, The Merciful...
*(recording inaudible)* to Allah (God) alone do I submit and seek refuge.
We thank Allah (God) for Moses and the Torah. We thank Allah
(God) for Jesus and the Gospel. We thank Allah (God) for
Muhammad and the Holy Qur'an.

I, as a student of scripture, thank Allah (God) over and over
and over again for raising up in our midst a divine leader, teacher,
and guide who has made the scriptures of the Torah, Gospel, and
Qur'an a meaningful plan of liberation for us and for all humanity. I
thank Allah (God) for the Honorable Elijah Muhammad. I hope and
pray that before too many days or years pass over you, that you also
will thank Allah (God) for the Honorable Elijah Muhammad. I greet
all of you, my dear Brothers and Sisters, with the greeting words of
peace in the Arabic language, we say, *As-Salaam Alaikum*! Peace be
unto you!

I want to thank the Sisters for handling the program today. I
thank you for the charity that all of you gave and thank you, my
daughter, for helping to raise. I thank the mistresses of ceremonies,
Sister Fabraye and Sister Charlene. and I thank Sister Ava for her
introduction of me. I thank Sister [Nicole] Evans, and I thank Allah
(God) for giving her such a magnificent instrument that she is using
for praise.

We are happy this afternoon, of course, to have my beloved wife who is the mother of my nine children, and grandmother of 22 and more on the way, Sister [Khadijah] Farrakhan. To all the mothers who are present today, we are very, very honored by your presence. To all the grandmothers and great grandmothers.

White America commercializes on everything. We know that none of us could get here without a mother. So, what a wonderful way to make a dollar—praise mother for a day. We can buy all kinds of lovely gifts for mother and think that we have done what we should have done by mother by giving her a bouquet of flowers or some little cheap expression of a card or some little gift. Maybe it's not a cheap expression, maybe it's a fine expression. But that's not the honor that mother should have. That is too cheap if it's only for 24 hours. That is too cheap. It is not a worthy expression for mother. In fact, every day that we live is a day to honor mother. Every day that we live.

This is Mother's Day. I'm excited. I've been excited all week thinking about today. I speak all the time but today was very special it seems to me. All week long, I was wondering and thinking about today. I want to thank my other daughter Maria and the florist for providing such a beautiful array of flowers. Most of them, you will have before the day is over. I don't know whether there's enough here for everybody. They're beautiful but not as beautiful as you. Flowers are magnificent, the way they beautify creation. But nothing beautifies creation like a woman. So, I'm excited about Mother's Day.

## Proper attitude toward women

How many of you are mothers? Would you raise your hands, please? No brothers raise your hand. All these wonderful mothers. I want to talk to you, Brothers and Sisters, about the value of mother. To all our Muslim Sisters who are present—if we all have to get up and give our guests our seats, we should be quick to do it because whatever we have, we built it for our people. If our people come in great numbers and we're put out of a seat, what a joyous thing.

What I want to say today about women, I want us to think and reflect on it, take it home and mull it over in your mind. Tomorrow morning when you get up, Brother, I'm hoping you will have a different attitude toward your mother and toward women. Sisters, when you take this message home and get up tomorrow morning, I hope you will have a different attitude towards yourself.

The attitude of women towards themselves is not a proper attitude. And certainly, the attitude of men toward women is not a proper attitude. We are disrespectful of ourselves. We are disrespectful of our women. We are disrespectful of our mothers. Many women are disrespectful of themselves because they really don't know who they are. You have a low opinion of yourself because you got your image of yourself not from God, but from corrupt men. There is no man who can give a woman the proper image of herself unless that man comes directly from God because God is your Creator. He knows why He created you. No one can give you your purpose better than God Himself.

## Oppressive religious misunderstanding

Have you noticed, Brothers, throughout the earth women are upset against men? Women are on the move in every society on the earth against certain rules that they feel are restrictive and oppressive. Women are revolting not just against oppressive conditions fostered by men, but men have fostered these conditions by their misunderstanding of religion. There is no religion on the earth that women are really happy with, in terms of their own self-expression.

For a long time in the church, women were not permitted to speak. Paul says [1 Corinthians 14:34] that women should be quiet. For many years, Paul held sway even over Jesus' attitude. Jesus is never seen in scripture rejecting women. He is seen as a protector, elevator, and teacher of women. The disciples were not like that. They were not assigned to women like Jesus.

Paul was very specific, that the woman shouldn't have anything to say in the church. It's strange, Sisters, that angels visited

35

women. Angels came to Mary. No angels have visited us, Brothers, have they? But angels visited Mary. But if Mary was in the church under that kind of teaching, Mary couldn't speak. She couldn't probably say what the angel told her because a man couldn't hardly hear it. In the Jewish tradition, women don't talk in the synagogue. In the Islamic tradition, women don't have too much to say. Not in the mosque. In fact, in the Islamic tradition many mosques don't allow the women in. Then they put that on God. We must get to the bottom of this.

We must understand if this is man's foolishness or did this come from God. If it came from God, then we want to know why. Are women intelligent? Yes. The Bible says [Proverbs 10:1] a wise child maketh a glad father, but a foolish child is the heaviness of its mother. Think about that. A wise child makes a glad father. If you have a wise child, isn't the father really happy? But father, you can't have a wise child unless you have a mother who is making the child wise. If a foolish child is the heaviness of its mother, then a wise child is the honor of its mother.

In this world, women are put down. She reflects all the attributes of God, but she can't move to bring out her attributes. She can't bring them out in the church. She can't bring them out in the society. Her space, or rather her place, has been the home. "Get in the home. Stay there. Don't come out until a man lets you out." She has all this talent and gifts that God gave her but she's not developing these gifts.

Is God prodigal? Did God waste time giving women all this talent and gifts and then confining women to the house? Then why is it that not only did Prophet Muhammad have women behind secure boundaries, but the Honorable Elijah Muhammad, our teacher, also put women first in the home? Is there something wrong with men? Are men threatened by intelligent women? If they are, something is wrong with the men because no real man is threatened by a strong woman. Any real man wants a strong woman, doesn't he? All praise is due to Allah (God).

## Woman is for man as earth is to humanity

I'd like to frame this subject saying that woman is for man as earth is to humanity. Woman is for man as earth is to humanity. If the earth is valuable, then woman is valuable. If we can't live without the earth, then we can't live without women. We call the earth "Mother." God created the earth for us. All of us come up out of it and all of us return to it. The earth must be protected in order for the earth to produce good crop. The earth must be protected. The Qur'an says [Surah 55:7] that God created the universe and He set the balance. God creates nature and God has set a balance in nature.

Since the Caucasian power, the earth has been corrupted. The African, the Native American, and ancient people knew how to live in harmony with the earth. New man evidently does not know how to live in harmony with the earth, so new man has corrupted the earth. Once you corrupt the earth, then everything produced from a corrupted is also corrupted. So, it is with the woman. If the earth today is corrupted, then woman is also corrupted because any man who does not respect the earth cannot respect women. Any man who will destroy the earth will destroy woman and will destroy himself. So, the whole planet is suicidal because of its treatment of the earth and its treatment of women.

God has given the earth protection. What is the protection for the earth? The Honorable Elijah Muhammad taught us that the atmosphere of the earth is made of fire. Any body falling into the earth's atmosphere is burned up on contact with the atmosphere. A protected environment. God loves the earth, so He protects it. Once you remove the protection from that which should be protected, then you start the process of corruption. The Qur'an teaches [Surah 30:41] "Corruption has appeared in the land and the sea on account of that which men's hands have wrought, that He may make them taste a part of that which they have done, so that they may return."

The earth now is corrupted. The sea is corrupted. You come from the earth. I come from the earth. Are we pure? How could we be if we don't have a pure foundation. The earth is now corrupted. The water is corrupted. The water and minerals of the earth make up your children. So, your children do not have a chance to really live because they come from a corrupted planet—corrupted not by the hands of woman. It says by men's hands.

Allah (God) created man. The Bible says [Genesis 1:27] in His own image, after His own likeness, but He gave man a duty. He said [Genesis 1:28], "multiply, and replenish the earth, and subdue it." God never gave man an instruction to corrupt the earth. He gave him an instruction to replenish it, repeople it, look after it, take care of it and bring it under the power of your knowledge. Subdue it. Replenish it. Take care of it. But what has man done? He has poisoned it.

## A poisoned earth

What kind of food are you eating? You are eating a poisoned food that has been denatured. Your whole body is dependent upon the chemistry of the earth to maintain itself. If the vegetables that you eat are denatured and de-powered, then they can't maintain this life. You are eating corrupted vegetables, corrupted fruit, and corrupted meat. You fish in the sea, but man has corrupted the sea. He put up factories that are poisoning and polluting seas, lakes, rivers, and oceans. When you pull a fish out the ocean, it looks like the same fish we used to eat but it's no longer the same quality. The fish is poisoned so when you eat it, you poison yourself. Why are you dying of cancer today in a modern world when 100 or 150 years ago your great-grandmothers and great-grandfathers never knew what cancer was, never had it, and never died from it?

There are more hospitals today in America because there are more diseases. There are more diseases than hospitals. More diseases than we have a place to care for the diseases. Why? The earth is corrupt. The sea is corrupt. They're talking now about the ozone layer. The ozone layer of the atmosphere keeps harmful rays of the sun from penetrating. Once you weaken the ozone layer, harmful rays of the sun get in and further poison the earth and its atmosphere. What does that have to do with mother?

Putting chemicals and pesticides into the earth poison the earth. When you pour water on the earth, the seeds germinate, and poison goes right into the seed. This is why the Honorable Elijah Muhammad taught us that you can't eat three meals a day. With the number of poisons that are in the best food, your bodies become a walking mass of poison. You never get a chance to cleanse because you don't know how to fast. You can purify the earth, you can purify the water, and you can purify your blood, but you must know how. This is a strange Mother's Day lecture, isn't it? "The man is talking about the ozone on Mother's Day."

Here are greedy men, pulling up trees and destroying the rainforests. "Oh, it's a tree. Pull it up. Cut it down. We must make a profit here." By destroying the rainforests, they're producing what they call the greenhouse effect, which is warming the earth and causing danger to those of us who live on the earth. The famine in Africa today is not God-made. It is man-made—made by greedy men who know but don't do better. They pull up trees. Trees protect the topsoil. When you pull up a lot of trees, the water comes and washes away the topsoil. When the topsoil is washed away, then the earth is no longer productive. The earthworm is valuable in creating topsoil. What does that have to do with mother?

Mother. "I didn't come here to get a lecture about the earth." I'm not talking just about the earth. I'm talking about you. Because the waters are poisoned, we are in serious trouble. We can live much longer than we are living but when you have a corrupted mother, a corrupted earth, that lessens your chance of survival.

Today, White folk have exploded nuclear devices under the ground. They've exploded nuclear devices on top of the ground, not realizing the effect that huge nuclear cloud would produce. They are building huge nuclear plants that have nuclear waste. They don't know what to do with their nuclear waste. So, they bury it. Where? In the earth. They bury it in so-called drums of steel.

But anything you put into the earth is not going to stay that way because the earth is a living thing. It is moving and shifting. It will break up steel over time. It will bring that steel right back to itself, in time. So, the earth is being poisoned and the poison of nuclear waste is getting into the water table. People are drinking poisoned water, eating poisoned vegetables and meats, and wonder why our bodies are wrecked with disease.

## Proper use of the earth

Poison in the Black community is doubled because they give you the worst food produced in the worst way. They say White people are living a little longer. White folks now die at 70 years of age while Black folks' life spans are getting short. Seventy years is nothing. Brothers, 70 isn't even a baby. Grandma, you haven't even reached the age to be considered a baby, and you're ready in your mind to check out. That's a shame. This shows you that we have never been taught how to live.

That's why, dear Christians, when the scripture says [John 10:10] that Jesus came that we may have life and have it more abundantly, I hasten to tell you in the most respectful manner maybe you have not met Jesus yet. Maybe you know his name and what he's going to do but maybe you haven't met him yet personally because you are dying too young. Seventy years of age and you're talking like you're an old man. "Well, I'm getting old now. I'm getting old, children. I don't have many more years." You're right—if you keep thinking like that, you won't have many more years.

If you open your Bible and read the genesis of these ancient patriarchs who lived 500, 600, 700, 800, 900, nearly 1,000 years, what is 70 years compared to 1,000? What is 100 years old compared to 600 or 700? You're losing your hearing, losing your sight, losing your faculties, and losing power over your body at such a young age. It is not because you're old; it's because Mother has been destroyed.

Mother. Native Americans could have taught White people a lot about caring for Mother Earth. Native Americans have a lot to teach the world about caring for the earth. The ancient Black people of the South and of Africa, they know what to do with herbs. They are not witchdoctors. They are herbalists of the highest form and expression. You think going to the drug store to get a pill is modern medicine. White folks are studying herbs. Then they synthesize the chemistry of the herb and put it in a capsule, and cause you to spend 20, 30, 40, 50, 60, 100 dollars for a capsule. But if you knew the earth and knew how to go to the earth, you would know that sickness is misuse of the earth. Your health and longevity are the proper use of the earth.

## In pure truth we purify ourselves

"Why are you talking like this, Farrakhan, on Mother's Day?" Any man who would corrupt the earth would also be a corruptor of women. When you have a corrupt woman, you can never produce the right kind of fruit from a corrupt tree. God doesn't put the weight of that on the woman. He does not. Many men like to point out, "That's a no-good woman." You hear it in the church. "Watch out for that woman. She'll trap you. She'll trick you with her guile and her cunning." If we're the men that we are supposed to be, she can't help but be the woman that she's supposed to be. Allah (God) says in the Qur'an [Surah 4:34] that men are the maintainers of women. Allah (God) never said that women are the maintainers of men. Allah (God) put that burden on men.

To maintain means to preserve, to protect, to keep safe. It was man's duty to keep the earth safe, preserve it, and protect it, but the earth is corrupted because the man who was given the job to preserve and protect it is a corrupted man. He's a rotten man. The men who have been given charge over you—woman—are as rotten and no-good as the men who were given charge over the earth. You have no preserver. You have no protector. You are a destroyed woman and that's why your children come back at you. When you think you've done good for them, they curse you to your face because you are a corrupt woman. Calling Jesus' name doesn't make you pure. Being in the church morning, noon and night doesn't make you pure. Running up and down the aisles getting the Holy Ghost doesn't make you pure.

Purity is gained through the knowledge of truth that is pure and we live up to that pure truth. In that truth, we purify ourselves. Allah (God) says [Surah 4:34] men are the maintainers of women. As I studied that, I said, oh my goodness, we have failed as men. We have failed our daughters. We have failed our wives. We have dishonored our mothers. What happened to us as men? We fell under the influence of a corruptor.

Our power to maintain her became broken by the corruptor. So, you are not the man that you and I should be, and she can't be the woman that she should be because it takes a man to make her that. God didn't make woman first. He made man first. So, Brothers, you are not going to remake the woman until you remake the man. God didn't say, "Let us make woman." He said, "Let us make man." According to the Bible, He makes man in His image and likeness. He gives the woman to the man. She's man's gift. If you have a gift and you don't know what to do with it, anybody will come and take your gift from you. That's just about what has happened.

## Protection

Polluted earth brings forth polluted life. Polluted water brings forth polluted life. Anything that is polluted does not have a chance for longevity. You say, "I had a grandfather who chewed snuff [tobacco]. He ate pork. He drank whiskey. He was something. He lived to 109." Imagine how long he would have lived if he didn't do that. So don't boast in your cheap, little years. Your little, cheap life span is nothing. Don't boast in that. The oldest one in here today hasn't even reached being a baby. The Bible, in the Book of Isaiah [65:20], says in that day a babe shall die one hundred years old.

My dear Brothers and Sisters, we are dying and haven't even learned the planet that we live on. It's almost a waste to come here and leave without doing something, leaving something of value to say that we were here. Before you can make your mark, you're gone. Why are you gone?

Hurt took you away. Alcohol took you away. Bad habits took you away. Where did you learn it? You learned it from the society. You learned it from your home. You learned it from your mother who learned it from a corruptor. Who is this corruptor?

Is religion really repressive of women? We can say yes, but why? Sisters, when you know your value, then you don't mind somebody putting protection on what is valuable. You don't protect something you don't value. You have a diamond ring. Somebody gave you a diamond? You gave it to yourself? Good. You're not going to go out on 47th Street and happen to just leave it. If it's worth something, you get to 47th Street and you turn it around and make it look like it's nothing. You have a gold chain around your neck. You'd better hide it when you get to 47th Street. Anybody who sees your valuables will take them. If you have sense, you put protection around them.

Do you have money? "I have a few dollars." I have a few, too. This is paper. Paper. How many people have gotten killed over this? How many homes have been broken up over this? How many families have fallen out because somebody died and left some of this to someone who we think they shouldn't have? Paper. Paper that somebody put a value on.

When you get paper, you take it to a bank and you say, "I am depositing this in my account." Why did you take it to a bank? Why didn't you keep it in your mattress? You say, I don't live in the right kind of neighborhood. These people will move my mattress out. So, I'm taking my money to a bank. I know they have steel vaults in there. They have guards with guns. So, I'm taking my money—which is paper—to a safe place.

What about your woman? She doesn't have any value to you. So, you let your woman roam the streets at night. Unprotected. Disrespected. "Have a good time baby! Come back when you get ready." What kind of a man is that? When you go home tonight and try to act like a protector, don't come back to me tomorrow and say she went upside your head. She is too magnificent to be left without protection. Do we protect the earth?

The Honorable Elijah Muhammad wrote in his book, "Message to the Blackman," the woman is man's field to produce his nation. That's a very heavy sentence. Some Sisters will say, "I'm not a man's field. Don't compare me to a field." Wait a minute, Sister. We just talked about the value of the earth. You are the producer of the people. If the people are no good, are you willing to take that responsibility that you aren't too good yourself?

You can't produce good unless you are good. You can tell a tree by what? The fruit it bears. What kind of fruit are you bearing, woman? If you are not bearing good fruit, how could you be a good woman? If you're not a good woman, where is your man? Where is the man?

## Maintainers of women

Don't get upset with me. This is a think tank subject. Brothers, Sisters, the Honorable Elijah Muhammad said, there's no such thing as a no-good woman. My God. I know what you're thinking. I didn't finish his sentence. The Brothers are thinking, "I know plenty of them." But the Honorable Elijah Muhammad said, "There's no such thing as a no-good woman. Every no-good woman was made no-good by a no-good man."

Brothers, if you become a corruptor, there's no way that a good woman will remain good in the hands of a corrupt man, particularly if she has fallen in love with the man. Sisters, your love becomes the instrument of your destruction when you love the wrong kind of man. You just seem to have a habit of falling in love with the wrong kind of man.

Somebody says, "I just love him. I can't help myself. I just love him." The man is beating you for breakfast, dinner, and supper but you're not leaving. "I have to stay right here because I love him. He brought something in the other day." What was it? "It was a little rock or something. He said, Honey, how do you feel? I said, I don't feel too good." He hasn't paid the rent in three months, but he will tell you "try some of this." Some of you Sisters will become drug addicts because your husbands are that. After he makes you a drug addict, he will make you a prostitute and bring men into your house because that lazy n—r doesn't want to go to work.

Men are the maintainers of women. A man cannot maintain a woman unless that man's connection with God is maintained. To maintain means to preserve, to protect, to keep safe. You can't preserve, maintain, protect, and keep safe a woman unless you are intact as a man.

## A set time for wicked rule

Do you know that Black people have built civilizations greater than the one you're living in now? Do you know that they are unearthing civilizations buried under the sands and the jungle that make this one look like kindergarten?

The Honorable Elijah Muhammad said to us, that when we knew 9,400 years before an enemy was coming, we prepared for him. Since he was going to rule, we covered up our wisdom, so that he would have to rule on the wisdom he was given and not on our ancient wisdom. You who are Masons, Shriners, and Eastern Stars, you who are wise know that the ancient study of masonry is the study of the wisdom of the Originator, which western man was only allowed 33 degrees of the wisdom of the Originator of a circle of 360 degrees of knowledge.

A Johnny-come-lately is going to come to the planet and his rule is limited. The Bible says [Genesis 3:22] that Adam, if he put his hands to the Tree of Life, he could become as God, or as we, and live forever. So, they kept him from that tree—it means knowledge. If the White man got a hold to a certain knowledge, you could never remove his civilization.

But God is so wise, He kept the great wisdom from this people so that when the time came for the end of their world, He would allow them to get a peek at wisdom that was far beyond their scope. When we knew that an enemy was coming, we buried our civilization under sand and jungle so that the new man would not gain the wisdom of our ancient civilization.

We would give him enough knowledge to run his world for 6,000 years. This is why the Honorable Elijah Muhammad taught us that he had a six-ounce brain. It didn't mean that his brain weighed six ounces. It meant that the weight of his knowledge would carry him 6,000 years. When the 6,000 years were up, his knowledge would be turned backward. He would become like a confused child because a greater knowledge would be introduced to break up the power of his knowledge.

Let's see if the Qur'an and the Bible bear witness to this. "I thank you, Father, Lord of heaven and earth, that you have hidden these things from the wise and prudent and revealed them to babes" [Matthew 11:25]. The wise and the prudent men who rule the world would not know what they should know to keep their world in the presence of a superior knowledge.

Allah (God) says in the Qur'an [Surah 2:30], "I am going to place a ruler in the earth." Then, the angels asked, "Wilt thou place in it such that will make mischief in it and shed blood?" Allah (God) said, "Surely, I know what you know not." God is going to allow someone to rule but the ruler is one who is going to be one who creates mischief and causes the shedding of blood.

Sisters, do you know what your nature is? The Honorable Elijah Muhammad said woman is created after the nature of God. She's the second self of man, and really the second self of God. Allah (God), created you to bow to Him. You're not man's woman. You're the woman of God. That's why men who don't have God in them can't keep you. Brothers, you may be handsome and that may get it for a minute. You may have big muscles and you may run down the football field, and she would drool and say, "Isn't he fine? He's so fine." That's the first stage. After "he is fine," you say, "I'm going to make him mine." When you go to make him yours, depending on what he wants, what you see is what you get. After he and you are married, there are many more handsome men than the man you married, and many more strong-looking, powerful-looking men. It has to be more than his good looks that keeps you.

Brother, do you know what keeps a woman? It is the wisdom of God in you and being dutiful to God so you will be dutiful to her. When you keep your duty to God and then are dutiful to the woman in terms of maintaining, preserving, and protecting her in the nature in which she is created, then God has deposited in her all the consolation that a man needs to make heaven on earth while you live. It's all in her.

The Honorable Elijah Muhammad said a woman is man's heaven. You said, "not mine." But Brothers, don't blame her. The Messenger said it's one thing to know that iron ore is in earth. It's another thing to mine it out and put it into the service of man. It's one thing to know that heaven is in the woman for us, but it is another thing entirely to extract it. You cannot extract it unless you become what God created you and me to be. "I'm going to place a ruler in the earth."

When you meet a man that you love, the first thing you do is submit to him. I'm not talking sex, I'm talking submission. When you love a man, when he says, "Honey, could you meet me at 8 o'clock," you lay that 8 in your brain. Around five, you're getting ready for 8. At 8, here she comes. You submit, honey. You're laughing. "Are you hungry?" You're hoping. You want to fix something for him even if you can't cook too well. You're trying to do something to please him. That's your nature.

If God says in the Qur'an [Surah 2:30], "I am going to place a ruler in the earth" but he's going to be a ruler to create mischief and cause the shedding of blood, then God must make provision for the woman because the first act of a ruler, if he's a wicked ruler, is to break the rule of the man. Once he breaks the rule of the man, the woman becomes his field to play around in. God knows that when the earth is corrupted, it can't bring forth good fruit. When the woman is corrupted, she can't bring forth good children. So, He said put the woman in the house, and lock your door.

Have you ever been a material witness in a court case? They will come to your house and take you like you are a criminal and lock you up. They'll say, "You are a material witness. Your testimony is germane to the success of the prosecution's case. Therefore, we cannot allow you freedom because they will kill you. So, we must put you in protective custody."

Protective custody looks just like jail, but the purpose is different. The motive is different. It's to keep you safe so you can give your testimony. God knew that a wicked one was coming to the earth to rule. So, you had to be put in protective custody in order for you to be able to produce the Messiah that one day would overturn the rule of an enemy of God.

I appreciate the changing of the post, but I think we ought to just sit down. It really attracts a lot of attention, and it takes away from the preaching of the Word. Everybody is sitting and not standing and falling out, we don't have to change post anymore. I'll be finished shortly. The Brothers are being trained and being made into real good soldiers. Isn't that a blessing?

Sisters, God wanted you protected. He tells the man, take your woman into the house, and keep her in her home. As her husband, you are the caretaker, preserver, and protector. You have to be on your watch for any corrupting influence coming into your home to your women. You don't let any strange man come to your woman. Strict orders from God—protective custody for the woman. How long will it last? As long as the enemy is on the planet, your woman has to be in protective custody.

You must understand this, Sisters. That's why religion seems so oppressive. It is not that God doesn't love you. It is because He loves you so much that He wants to keep you as safe as He can keep you, so that perhaps one of your wombs will produce the one who would bring about the end of this world, salvation, and the bringing in of a new reality. Isn't that beautiful? There's so much to this. We can't say everything in a short period of time. You are smart enough to take the germs of what we're saying and look more deeply in it.

## Who is the enemy?

All throughout scripture women have had to be placed in a certain way. Why? The enemy is coming. Who is the enemy? You may not like it, but it is the Caucasian male, his way of civilization. You may not like this. It may seem "not religious" to you, but the White man's way is alien to God. He has created a world of disorder, mischief, and blood-shedding. He loves to get into your woman. Am I lying?

Brothers, the White man will come into every nation. After he breaks the man of that nation, he goes after the woman. When he gets the woman in his clutches, he feeds her, teaches her, corrupts her, then mixes his blood in her so that the children that she produces will really be his children. They won't be God's children. They will be bastards—meaning that they are the offspring of a ruler who came to earth to bring about disorder. You can't bring about disorder until you corrupt the woman after you break the power of a man to be her maintainer, preserver, and protector.

Sisters, this man can't command you, this poor Black man. We have been made so pitiful, Brothers. The Black woman wants to be with us, but at a great price. You can't control her because you don't have enough knowledge. She's smarter most of the time than the men, so you get into a lot of arguments. The only way you can get some order in the house is to beat her up. And you do that quite often. Men don't beat women. If you have to beat a woman, you don't need a woman.

The enemy has broken us as men. Our woman has been a field for him, and that's why I'm this color. If I were truly African, I wouldn't look like this. What happened to the slave man? He was broken as a man. Once you make a man a slave, he's through. He can't protect her. He doesn't have any power to protect her. He's a slave. So, she becomes the prize. He goes into you and produces offspring. He doesn't want to nurture those offspring and he really doesn't want you to be a good, strong mother. So, he corrupts you and he uses you. You don't teach your children the way of God because you really don't know God's way. You teach your children the foolishness that you learned from this foolish world.

Mother. You don't really know what to do with your baby. You have them but you don't know how to rear them. You were never taught how to rear them. Don't get angry with me. Please don't. Don't get angry with me. This is Mother's Day. I'm not trying to make you angry. I'm just trying to tell you the truth. If you knew what to do with your children, you would have made a better child.

Some of us are better than others at mothering. Sometimes it's a natural instinct. Maybe God has given it to you as a blessing. Some of you have strong parents and they passed on good things to you, so you did better than others. But none of us have come up to where God wants us. We have all fallen short of the glory of God. Dear Sisters, this is not a putdown. Please don't take it like that.

You're teaching your children foolishness. You sit in front of the television all day if you have cable. You're looking at the latest dances or foolish soap operas. You're not sitting with your children, putting wisdom in their heads. You have them learning the latest dance. "Come on, baby. Come on, honey. Shake it for me. Show me how you do it." If they see you shaking all the time, what are they going to do? Shake like mama shakes. If they see you baking all the time, they'd bake like mama bakes.

If you don't know how to make a home, you can't teach children to make what you don't know how to make. Beloved Sisters, the enemy has destroyed us as men so we can't be to you what we should be. He's corrupted our women so you can't bring forth children like you should. So, we are all dead—mentally, morally, spiritually—and in need of being resurrected to divine spiritual life.

## Making better men

To the pastors who are present, to the imams who are

present, to the great leaders of religions who may be present or advocates of religion, if you look at what you're doing, you're not really producing good fruit. You're maintaining the status quo of a world of disorder. If a Muslim man doesn't want his wife to come to the masjid, she doesn't pray with you; you pray for her. You are not fit to teach her. You really don't know how to teach her. You want to be her teacher but haven't been taught yourself. You have a dissatisfied woman.

She builds the church that she can't talk in. There's not a church that has been built that wasn't built by women. If women can build the church, how come they can't preach in the church? Without the women, the pastor is finished because there are no men there to help the pastor build the church. The men are in the street; the women are in the church.

The White man gives her jobs. He has to give it to a minority, so he'd rather give it to a minority woman than to a Black man. So, he gets you, Sisters. You're working downtown, your husband is walking uptown without a job. You dress up in fine suits and go downtown working for White folks while the man who gives you babies has no job even if he has a college degree. They will say he's overqualified or too qualified for a job or doesn't have enough experience or qualifications, so they won't give him a job.

The poor man comes home to you. You're already working. You say, "Well, darling, don't worry. I'll do the best that I can for us both." What does that do for his self-respect? There's no man living that's a real man who wants his woman working for him. There's no real man alive who can sit and look at his children without decent clothes to wear because he doesn't have a job.

Naturally sex is a part of our life. Sex is a part of nature. When we have sex, we produce children, but every child is another burden on a head that can't work in the white man's world. The more he looks at you in your condition and looks at his babies, he says, "I can't handle it" so he walks out the door. That's why 70 percent of Black homes are headed by a woman. There is no man present because the church, mosque, synagogue, and schools have failed to produce a Black man. A Black man who is connected to God isn't dependent on the White man to make a job for us. If you and I have come to God, God will give us the strength to rely on Him.

There are worms for the birds to eat, and food for the fish, and vegetation for everything to eat, yet we—the greatest of God's creation—must walk around and look for a cheap handout at a church door when we have heads and hearts and hands and feet that can work. No. A woman can't respect a man who does not have any ability to provide for her. It's not in her nature to continue to love you without any money. You say, "Baby, you took the vow. You said for better, for worse." It's worse but it's not getting any better. That's the problem. It's not our fault, Brothers, but we are going to have to stop this. We're going to have to break into the cycle and break it up.

Somebody must break into the cycle of corruption of our women and make a better woman. When you make a better woman by making a better man, you'll make better children who will bring in a better world. That's what we want. We want a better world for our children. There's not going to be a better world until there's a better you. And there won't be a better you until God makes a better man for you. Even if the man isn't right yet, God always was and is right. Since you are the woman of God, then you must tie back up to God as a direct source for your life, Sisters. Clean and purify yourself from the corruption of the White man's world so that you can become like a mother like mothers have never been before.

**The cornerstone of the home**

Where do you begin to end the corruption of the earth? It begins with knowledge. Scripture says [Hosea 4:6], "My people are destroyed for lack of knowledge." You have been a free-for-all kind of woman. When you were in the South on the farm, you did better. You produced your food. Do you remember? You churned your butter. Do you remember? You watched the chickens as they laid their eggs. You took fresh eggs and fed yourself and your family. You didn't have a lot of money, but you had health, better than you have today. Now, we're so dependent on White folk for everything. They are corrupting everything that we eat. This is why the Honorable Elijah Muhammad said we have to have land of our own in order to build a new reality. I want the Sisters to understand the Honorable Elijah Muhammad.

The Honorable Elijah Muhammad was not an ordinary teacher. If he were an ordinary teacher, he would produce ordinary students. He was an extraordinary teacher. How do you know he is an extraordinary teacher? By what he taught and his example. He was taught by a Master, there's no question about that. The One who taught the Elijah Muhammad taught him how to eat to live, first by purifying the food.

When my wife and I became Muslim, one of the first things we heard was, "No aluminum pots." I didn't know about cooking in an aluminum pot. It was a pot. You have to cook in something. We cooked in the pots. The Elijah Muhammad said no, get rid of the aluminum pot. You cook in stainless steel. We didn't ask why, we just obeyed. Come to find out now that traces of aluminum get in your food and poisons your system. You have brain damage after you eat a lot from these aluminum pots. It's not that you're old. You're not old, you just didn't know how to eat to live. The Honorable Elijah Muhammad started teaching us.

He said to the Sisters, "You have to know how to make a home. Come into the house." Naturally, intelligent, highly developed women find that insulting. "Me? Not me. I'm just too intelligent for that." He started a movement, but he didn't base it on Sisters with a Master degree or Ph.D. degree. A very unhappy woman you are, with all your degrees but you don't have a man. Those degrees can't keep you warm at night. None of your professional degrees can make you happy in your home. You can't take that degree home with you and wrap it around yourself and say, "I am happy, child, with my B.S. degree." No. Nobody is ever happy with bs—I mean degree. If you don't know how to make a home, you don't know how to be a happy woman. You will never be a happy woman until you know how to make a home. That's where it all begins—in the home.

Everything starts in the home and the woman is the cornerstone of family. She's the cornerstone of home. In righteous circles, we don't shack up. We just don't do that. "Oh, that's my man over there." Oh, you're married? "No, no, no. We have an understanding. We're just shacking up." No, no, no. No, no, no. You have a shacking up understanding?

You must make a man commit himself. What marriage is today is really a shacking-up. People aren't serious. That's why I don't like to say weddings. I say funerals because they're serious. I know when they are dead, they are dead. They're not lying about being dead. That's why I say funerals. I know he's dead. When we put him away, I know he's put away.

But when you come before an altar, talking about "I will" and you mean you won't, "I do" and you mean you don't—I don't like to be involved in that kind of madness. I don't like to be involved in lies and shack-up relationships. You get in it for five minutes. When you run into a little snag, you get out of it and leave a woman, now pregnant with a baby. You don't have any understanding of what life is. I don't like to be involved in that. I hate irresponsible men. Their words mean nothing in the presence of God or to their mate or to themselves. I hate that. All we have when we enter into marriage is our word. If our words mean nothing, then we are nothing.

Marriage is the cornerstone of a family. That's why God killed people when they commit adultery because adultery breaks up the cornerstone of family. Family is the cornerstone of nation. Anything that breaks up a family is destroying a nation. To kill an individual is preserving the nation. That's why God kills individuals when they break His law. I know this is rough.

The Honorable Elijah Muhammad said to the Sisters, "Come in, Sisters." He said go in your homes and I want you to make your home the most wonderful place for you to live. Come in the home, Sisters. Why? There is a corruptor out there. We don't want you any more corrupted than you are. We want to purify the woman, so that if we purify the woman and the man, we get a product that will purify the world.

## Standard of civilization

The Honorable Elijah Muhammad said, Sisters, you have to learn how to cook. Some of you don't know how to cook right. You have no time to cook. That's why McDonald's is killing you. Burger King, Wendy's, McDonald's, Church's—I hope they don't sue me. That's what you're feeding yourself. That's what you're feeding your children. You're killing yourself and your children with this greasy, no-good food because you don't have any time.

It takes time to make a home. The economics of today's world means both husband and wife must work. Husband and wife must work but you're having children. Who is rearing the children? "I don't know. I put them over here at this daycare center." They're playing wild sex games at the daycare center. "I put them over here." Somebody who doesn't care for your children is rearing your children. You must work because there is not enough money.

When the Honorable Elijah Muhammad was here, we, men worked, and our wives reared our children. We, as men, would provide whatever was needed to make that family work. The Honorable Elijah Muhammad was not enslaving her. He was putting the woman in protective custody.

When he told you, Sisters, to lower the hem of your garments, he didn't want any men looking at your legs, thinking that you were legs instead of an intelligent creation of God. He said, ease up on the dress, don't make it so tight. What are you trying to fashion? Ease up. Why ease up?

You're so fine, you want to show your finery. That's why men are like dogs today. You're helping to make a dog out of a man by showing him what will make him lust for you rather than really love you. Just loosen up a bit. You can be beautiful. You don't have to cut the neck of your dress down so low.

The Honorable Elijah Muhammad was a civilizer. You don't civilize by the standard with men. Women are the standard by which you judge the degree of civilization of a people. The Honorable Elijah Muhammad taught us to fight for you. No question about it. Anybody tries to mess over you, that was death. We would carry it out. We didn't care who it was—white, black, didn't make any difference. You don't play with our women. That's the way it is in the Muslim world.

In our world, you don't let men come in your home, looking for your woman. Someone knocks on your door, and they come in. You're the man of the house. They're supposed to be coming to see you. "Where's your wife?" Why do you want to know where my wife is? Did you come to see me or my wife? In the Islamic world, it's a great honor to you if a man even presents his wife to you. In that world, they don't present their wives to you at all.

They're serious about God, knowing that a wicked one was coming. They're going to put some protection on their women. Not only do they dress her up and cover her so that you can't see her wares, some went totally out of the box and put veils on them. When they walk the street, you can't whistle because you don't know what you're whistling at. She walks by you, and you see something moving but you don't know what it is. "Yeah, that's my wife." If you say the wrong thing, you won't need a dentist. You will see the undertaker.

That's why when American soldiers went into the Islamic world, one of the first things they taught them was to leave the Muslim woman alone. These people will kill you over their women. That's the way we must be again. We must be killers if it's necessary to protect our women.

You say, that's not righteous. Oh, yes, it is. I will stand before any judge in America. "Did you kill that man?" Yes, I killed him. "It's against the law." Maybe so, but it's against the law for this man to try to corrupt my wife and my house. I'll kill the weeds that try to corrupt my crop. I'll kill the insects. I'll put a scarecrow on my land. I'll get a shotgun. If I see any man trying to steal my crop, I will blow him away. Isn't that right, Your Honor? We would have a field day in the court. All we have to do is stand up. We'd make a new law. We must protect our women.

Sisters, as I looked at this subject, I said religion is repressive, not because God wanted it to be. God knew that an enemy was coming and that that enemy would corrupt the woman. He put you in the vanguard position as a protector of your family. We have failed in that duty and the White man has conquered as men. Our women are no longer ours. They want to be, but they're not ours.

## The value of virtue

I thank Allah (God) for the Honorable Elijah Muhammad. He taught us the parables from the New Testament. I'll close with the parable of the wicked husbandmen [Matthew 21:33-46; Mark 12:1-12; Luke 20:9-19]. The earth was let out to be controlled by some wicked husbandmen. The earth—women—would be under the control of wicked men. God sent persons to check the fruit. Some, the wicked husbandmen beat; some, they killed; some, they put in prison. But when the heir to the vineyard came, the wicked husbandmen utterly slew the heir. Jesus asked the Jews what will the lord of the vineyard do when he comes? The Jews answered saying he will utterly slay the wicked husbandmen [Matthew 21:40-41; Mark 12:9; Luke 20:15-16].

In scripture, the vineyard represents the earth. You can see that the wicked have corrupted the earth. Every now and then, God will send a prophet into the world to check the product of the wicked rulers. The product was as corrupt as the rulers. So, God's prophets always had to reform people. The enemy did not like a reformer among the people. Some, they beat; some, they imprisoned; some, they killed. That's the history of the prophets.

Today, we have been in the hands of a wicked people. They have broken us as men, and they have corrupted our women. From them, we are corrupt men who do not know how to be real men. Our poor mothers are in pain because of us. They love us but they don't necessarily know what to do for us. That's why we thank Allah (God) for the Honorable Elijah Muhammad. Moreso than anybody, that man understood what to do for us.

I remember one day when he got this building. We were driving in the car together. The Honorable Elijah Muhammad said he was going to build a fence around this property, like a wall that you couldn't see in it. He said, now I can let my children out of prison.

Some of you Sisters—my daughters were among them, my daughters Donna, Betsy Jean, and Maria—were the foundation of the University of Islam in New York City. They were sacrificed in a sense. Elijah Muhammad told me, take your children out of the public school and I did. They grew under Islamic training. It wasn't the high-towered education of some of the finer schools, but it was a God-centered education. Some of you who grew up in the University, you didn't even know the value of what the Honorable Elijah Muhammad was giving you until you didn't have it anymore. Some of you, like my daughters, wanted to go to college. They had completed high school.

The Honorable Elijah Muhammad said, "Don't send them." What do you mean, Dear Apostle, don't send my girls? They want to grow in knowledge. He said, "Don't send them. Wait until I build a university where we will have a dormitory for 10,000 students. Tell them wait." Why wait, Sister? He knew that you wanted knowledge and that you needed knowledge, and he wanted you to have it. But he had made you virtuous girls. You went off into life a virgin. There's no such thing as a virgin in this world. You don't know the value of what a virtuous woman is.

It is better for you to not have a degree and have your virtue than to be a degreed whore. I know it's hard. You can never get your virtue back once it's gone. You can always grow in knowledge. But knowledge must be supported by character. The White man's world doesn't build character. It gives you knowledge, but you are a low-life people. Knowledgeable low-life men and women. The White man isn't thinking about building a better world. But the Honorable Elijah

Muhammad was. He wanted his women and girls protected because when you don't have any decent women, you'll never produce a decent man.

## Good fruit from a good tree

That man, that man, Elijah Muhammad. When you say his name, you ought to say all praise is due to God that at last God gave us a man, not the White man gave us a man. God gave us a man, a man for all seasons. Excuse me for raising my voice and getting excited. I get angry when I think of you, my dear Muslim Brothers and Sisters. We love Prophet Muhammad. We can't be Muslims if we don't love the man through whom the Qur'an was revealed. But Prophet Muhammad has been dead for 1,400 years and he doesn't have good representation in the Islamic world.

Nobody came after us. Nobody cared for us. But Master Fard Muhammad came and raised up one from us for us. Nobody can teach Black America like Elijah Muhammad. And nobody in Black America can teach Black people like his student, Louis Farrakhan. I am the teacher today. I'm not trying to blow a horn on myself. I am a teacher from the Honorable Elijah Muhammad to civilize Black men and women so that you will be accepted and respected throughout the world.

Elijah Muhammad wrote the parents of a Sister who said they were sending her to college, and told them, send her but if anything happens to your daughter while she is in these dens of iniquity, then I will double the punishment to you. He made us protectors of our family, yet we turned our family over to these dens of filth. What do you think these dens of filth are going to make of our women and girls? They go there one way, and they come back another. The White man's world is not going to produce a good product.

That's why without Mary, you never would have had Jesus. You could not have had a Mary unless there was a Zacharias. Zacharias was the man in whom Mary was placed in his charge. Brothers, until we become decent men, where our girls in our charge will not be molested by us, you will never make a decent product. A good woman must grow under good men. That's why Elijah Muhammad set up a woman's class and wouldn't let a man go near it. He threatened us with punishment if we tried to dabble in the women's class. Why? Because there is no man worthy.

### True and responsible motherhood

Mothers, when you leave here today, look at yourself. Look in the mirror at yourself. You are God's representative to your children. You are not man's representative. You are God's representative to your children. We come out of the darkness of your womb, even as He brought all creation out of the darkness of space. He makes your womb after His own laboratory of creation. He makes you loving and compassionate as a mother. Although there are women today doing things that you'd never would have thought you'd ever see—having babies and throwing them into incinerators, flushing them down toilets, throwing them out windows, burning them up in ovens. We have truly become animals.

I plead with you, Sisters, when you leave this place, you are potentially the best friend and teacher to all human beings. When a true mother is lost, that is a pain you never get over. My mother passed away approximately 18 months ago. I didn't know how powerful my mother was. It's something that you take for granted because she's there all the time. When my mother was no longer present, it was like someone took a warm blanket away from me.

For the first time, I felt a chilly wind because my mother was a divine protector for me as you, mothers, are divine protectors for your children. Fathers don't wake up instinctively in the middle of the night. God puts that in you. When your little ones are suffocating, somehow you know it and wake up in the night to save your baby in time. It's you, mother.

You're the greatest friend that God has given to living beings. As great as a father is, there is nothing and no one like a mother. Prophet Muhammad was moved to say that heaven is at the feet of mothers. Prophet Muhammad was moved to say that he who treats his mother best is best among you.

You that raise your voice to your mother, from this day forward—never again. If your mother is alive today, go find her. If you are angry with her for whatever reason you may think you're justified, there is no reason that the Qur'an gives that justifies us being disrespectful to our mothers. So, find your mother, embrace her, and thank her for doing the best that she could, even if it wasn't too good. She brought you here and without her you could never have been.

Young mothers, fill your head with knowledge. Your mother did the best she could. Now you can't boast or say that you did not have sufficient knowledge because now God is flooding us with greater knowledge. If you want it, you can get it and use it to build strong life. My mother was not a high school graduate. My mother was not a college graduate. My mother was a very wise Black woman, wise with common sense.

Most of you, our mothers, didn't get a college education. You didn't hardly get a high school education. You came from the South where you worked hard day in and day out. You didn't have a chance to get it, but you tried to make sure your children got it. But your children with education have not accomplished what you have accomplished without it. Haven't you worried about that? They have all these degrees and are less productive. Not all, but most.

Sisters, young mothers, imbue yourself with knowledge. Stop being silly women and start being serious women. Life is serious, not silly. It's not frivolous. When you have children, you have responsibility. The more you grow here (points to his head), then when you teach your baby, you take the wisdom from here and you put it in their little ears. In a few days, you'll see your children acting like children of wisdom. The way you start today: Clean up your bodies. Don't put any filth knowingly in this House of God.

Don't snort any cocaine, Brothers, because the cocaine you snort today that messes up your brain will affect the sperm that is the future of our people. If you're coked up, you've coked up your sperm. If you're coked, Sister, and you have a baby growing in you; you're smoking cigarettes and you have a baby growing in you; you're drinking whiskey and you have a baby growing in you—no! Up to today, OK. After today, no good.

"How do I stop? How do I stop? I want to stop." Stop. "Is it that easy?" No. You must make up your mind. You don't need pills. You don't need hypnosis. You don't need that. Do you know what you need? You need to develop your will, not a pill. Your will. When you say, "I won't"—mean it. Throw the cigarettes away. Throw the alcohol and drugs away after today. Do not defile your house. On Friday nights, we have study groups. We're dealing with the study of how to develop the power of our own beings to be able to command what we want out of life and not be beggars. Every Muslim, every visitor, you should be at that Friday class. Don't miss it.

Thank you for your attendance. Thank you for your attention. No longer corrupt the earth because, when you corrupt the earth, you corrupt yourself. Thank you for listening. May Allah bless you as I greet you in peace. *As-Salaam Alaikum!*

# 4 A NATION CAN RISE NO HIGHER
# THAN ITS WOMAN

In The Name of Allah, The Beneficent, The Merciful. the One God to Whom all praise is due, the Lord of the worlds. We thank Allah (God) for His Coming in the Person of Master Fard Muhammad, to Whom praise is due forever, and for His intervention in our affairs, raising up in our midst a Divine Leader, Teacher and Guide, the Messenger of Allah, His Messiah to us, the Most Honorable Elijah Muhammad. I greet all of you, my dear and wonderful Sisters, with the greeting words of peace. We say it in the Arabic language, *As-Salaam Alaikum*!

My dear Sisters, I am very, very thankful to Almighty God for blessing us with this privilege of being able to speak with you for just a few moments of your time. I have been stressed for two days. This has never happened to me before, thinking about talking to you. You might ask, "Why should you be stressed, Farrakhan? You do this all the time." Yes, but there never was a time that I have spoken to an audience of women only.

The Honorable Elijah Muhammad never let men enter or become a part or familiar with the women's class in the Nation of Islam. The women of the world have been destroyed by men. The Honorable Elijah Muhammad said to me that there's no such thing as a no-good woman. There is no such thing as a no-good woman.

Wherever you find a no-good woman, there's a no-good man who made her that way.

Because of your sacredness, he did not want men interfering with the development of a class of righteous women. He wanted to provide a sanctuary, a place where women were safe that they might grow into the women that God intended. So, he didn't want any man interfering with that development.

On two occasions in New York City, he permitted me to enter the woman's class. He gave me what he wanted me to say. As ministers, we were threatened by him that if we messed up with this class, that would be the end of our ministry and we would be out of the Nation. So, when I went in the class, I approached it with trepidation. And it's that same feeling that I have tonight. You are more than who you think you are. Therefore, any man who has the honor to speak to you, and knows who he is speaking to, should approach you with fear and trepidation.

I intended to have a women-only meeting, but I didn't know when. I've been touring the country, speaking to Black men because the Black man is in deep, deep trouble. When I was in Atlanta to speak to Black men only, I came out a shoe store. Some Brothers and Sisters were standing outside to greet me. One Sister walked out the crowd and said, "Brother Farrakhan, you're speaking to men only but we need someone to talk to us. When are you going to speak to women?" I said to her, "God willing, I'll be back in 30 days." I want to ask that Sister to stand because, without her, it might not have been Atlanta. Tammy, come on up. I want them to see you. Escort her, please. We ought to give her a hand because it was her suggestion. Let's hear it for Sister. It's wonderful to make your word bond. I promised her that I would come back and I'm back. I'm honored to be here to speak with you.

I want to thank everyone who spoke before me. I want to thank Reverend Barbara King. She had to leave. She's speaking somewhere tomorrow morning and she had a flight to catch. I want to thank Sister Ava Muhammad for her words. Thank you for your charity. It cost us quite a bit to put this on but there is no amount of money that's more valuable than one of you. I'd like to prove that to you before this night is over.

## Women are co-operators with God

Who are you? What makes you so special? Sisters, you have carried us, not only in your wombs. You have carried us on your backs for 400 years. God has come to relieve you of that burden and make a man for you that you will be proud to honor and respect. Your suffering is great as Black women. You're suffering is inordinate. The only way you could make it is if God walked with you. If there is no God, then the weight of what you carry would destroy you.

You, the Black woman, have had to bear the burden of being torn away from our native land and people, and carried on ships through the Middle Passage. You have had to see your man broken. This is not an accident that you are without a proper mate today. That is by design.

The enemy has destroyed the Black man so that the Black man cannot be to you what God intended. This keeps you from being what God intended. When you listen to our women speak, our women speak of pain. They speak of suffering. They speak of hurt. They speak of being betrayed. When you listen to our men speak, they speak of their suffering, their pain, and their hurt. Each one of us is looking to the other as the cause of the problem, when neither the Black man nor the Black woman is the cause of the problem. But a house divided against itself cannot stand. Your burden has been great, but there's a God Who was involved in your suffering.

There is so many things I want to share with you. Time is short so I want to move quickly, but not without care. If I'm moving too fast, I would hope that my wife or Sister Tynnetta Muhammad would slow me down because I don't want you to miss one word.

You are a sacred individual, more than you know. The secret of God Himself is bound up in you. The world is in trouble because the world has no respect for the woman. If the world has no respect for women, the world has no respect for God. When you respect God, you must respect women because the womb of the woman is a place of sacredness. It should be reverenced and held in awe. Even a thought, not of worshipping women, but women should be held in awe because of the majesty of her womb. When God and woman co-operate, Jesus comes forth, Moses comes forth, and Abraham comes forth. Greatness comes forth when God and woman cooperate.

When women are estranged from God, then the womb produces a bitter fruit. Women must be reconnected to God so that the fruit of your wombs will once again be the kings, rulers, and masters of every discipline, whether it is male or female coming from your wombs. These are the fruit of God.

Sisters, we live in a world that has put the woman down. No religion is free from some blame. Not that God did this, nor did God's prophets do this. Misunderstanding and misinterpretation of scripture has caused males in religious positions to put the female down, justifying their mistreatment of the woman by talking about what Eve did. Eve could not do anything more than what Adam permitted so it never was Eve's fault.

To say that God created man, then put man to sleep and took a piece, man's rib—if you are made from a rib, you are made inferior. That is not so. Scriptural scientists, we need to talk about the real meaning of that. It has good meaning but to apply it to women is wrong; to apply it to the female is not quite right.

Let me talk to you about where you came, from who you came from, and why you are here. The Qur'an says [Surah 4:1], "O people, keep your duty to your Lord, Who created you from a single being and created its mate from the same essence, and from these two spread many men and women."

Think about this. Allah (God) says in the Qur'an that He created man from a single being and created woman from the same essence. What is the essence of man and what is the essence of woman? The essence of man and woman from which we come is

66

God Himself. You are not the woman of man. You are the woman of God.

## Heaven on earth

Think about yourself. Look around you. Who are the persons in the Black community who are the seers? It's not the men. Who is it that will tell you something about your future? Most of the time is who? It's you. Why? Why do you see sometimes better than the preacher—most times—but yet you are not supposed to preach? How is it you could produce the greatest human being who walked the earth—Jesus the Messiah, produced from a woman who taught him and nurtured him. If you could teach Jesus, shape and mold him, what other man is it that you cannot shape and mold?

Sisters, you are a direct descendant of God. You are more than sisters from your mother's womb. It's bigger than that. The sister sitting next to you, that's your Sister in the real sense of the word, not just from the womb of your mother. She's your Sister from the womb of God. The Honorable Elijah Muhammad taught me that you are older than the sun, moon, and stars. He said God's first act of creation after creating Himself was to create a woman to console and comfort Him.

I want to talk to you about your nature. Since you came from God, you are not equal to God. You are just a little less than He, but you are from Him. Whatever characteristics are in God and in man are also in you. Read Genesis 5:2 carefully: "Male and female created He them; and blessed them and called their name Adam." Adam is not just a man. Adam is representative of a people, male and female. If Adam is made in the image and likeness of God, that's not just man, that's you (woman). In the image of God, in the likeness of God with the brain to envision and create with wisdom from God. You are more than what you have been made to believe. What happened? What happened?

The Honorable Elijah Muhammad taught us that the nature of the woman is that of a consoler. Look at the word "console."

When someone needs to be consoled, someone must speak the right word to your mind, present the right picture, create the right atmosphere to bring about consolation. Is that all woman is here for? No. The Qur'an says [Surah 30:21] God created the woman that the man may find peace and quiet of mind in her. There is no heaven for a man outside of you. Woman is the real heaven of man. Man is the real heaven of a woman. When man and woman operate under the Will of God, we create heaven on earth. That's why you pray, "Our Father which art in heaven. Thy Will be done on earth as it is in heaven." That will never happen until the woman and the man are made right again. Jesus said [Luke 17:21] the Kingdom of God is where? within you.

### Every woman should be educated

Sisters, have you noticed the type of man that appeals to you? Certainly, being physical, you look for something physically attractive. Probably mistake number one. "Child, he sure is fly." That's a beginning. When he is attractive to you, what is it that you feel inside for him?

First, God created you as a consolation for someone who is a worker and a producer. You don't have the spirit to console someone that's doing nothing. I don't care how handsome the Brother may be. After a while, good looks look ugly if the man is not producing.

God created you to help the man do God's Will. That's why in the Bible [Genesis 2:18], you are called a helpmeet. It did not say mate. It said meet. Not m-e-a-t. M-e-e-t. Help meet what? God laid on man in his nature the responsibility to do what? God gave man dominion over the fowl of the air, the fish of the sea, and every creeping thing that crawls [Genesis 1:26]. God told man to multiply, replenish the earth, and subdue it [Genesis 1:28]. He put woman there to help the man to meet what God had put on man to do.

If the man is doing nothing, then how can you help a man do nothing. When you meet a man—he's handsome, he's good looking, he's beautiful, he has a good rap. Then you ask him, "What are you doing?" *I ain't doing nothing.* "Where are you going?" *I ain't going no place.* Why do you want to be bothered with someone who's going nowhere, doing nothing. That's not who you are. That's why most of you are unhappy women. That's why you get married and divorced so quickly. Something is missing in the marriage, and you don't quite understand what it is. It's not the man's fault. Sisters, don't blame him. He's not going to be the man that he *could* be unless you help him to become the man that he *should* be.

For him to be that kind of man, you must know who he is, know who you are, and then, above all, know how to move him to the goal that God wants him to reach. You must know how to do that otherwise he will be living in your mouth like a dentist.

Sisters, you know you are suffering from great abuse. There's hardly a woman in this audience who hasn't been beaten by a man. Although some of you are get pretty tough—you're beating up your husbands nowadays—none of that should be necessary. In this world, the White male could not stand for the Black male to have power and dominion. So, the White male broke the Black male so that he is power-less, without dominion. Once your man is broken, you become fair game for the victor. In war, they call it the spoils of war or booty.

Sisters, that is what the Black woman has become to the slave masters' children. You are the booty or the prize. He has access to you because he has conquered and destroyed your man. Then you will sing songs, "Shake your booty!" You will do dances that suggest that that's who and what you are. In the 1960s, singing groups called themselves "The Supremes." Supreme meaning the highest. Today, our women call themselves, "bitches with problems" and "whores with attitudes." We have accepted that. That shows you how far our women have fallen.

If a nation can rise no higher than its woman and women are looked at as bitches and whores, and this is accepted in the society, then the nation has gone to hell because they have lowered the woman down. The nature of you is to console a productive man. The nature of you is to speak to his mind that which consoles him in his effort to do God's Will. To say that a woman should not be educated is foolishness.

Every woman should be knowledgeable because a wise woman makes a wise nation. A foolish woman makes a foolish people. To keep women ignorant, looking at soap operas all day long, feeding their minds filth and ignorance is to keep you in a state where you will never produce children who will be masters and conquerors. You will always be a conquered people because your woman has been made a foolish woman.

## Freedom and balance

The slave masters have put us in a condition from which only God can get us out. So, Brother Farrakhan has been touring the country, talking to Black men. In the beginning God said [Genesis 1:26], "Let Us make man." Unless a good man is made for you, you will feel like you feel now—unloved and unwanted. You have beautiful children but no father to look after your children. You feel unloved but then are called upon to give love to your children. How can you give what you don't receive?

You have done an excellent job with your children with hardly anything to go on. You must ask yourself, "Why did this happen to us? Did God know about this? If so, why did God permit a whole people to be destroyed?" Not for a day, not for a year but for four centuries and for the last 6,000 years, Black people have not really had their day in the sun. Why God? What has happened?

Sisters, according to the Qur'an [Surah 4:34], the woman should always be protected. When you have money, you try to put it in a safe place. When you have jewelry, you don't leave your jewels out for the thief to steal. You are more valuable than all the gold that is in the earth. You are a great treasure than any treasure that can be found in the depths of the sea.

But today, you are unprotected. No wise man will leave his woman unprotected. God knew that Satan was going to come into power in the earth. If an enemy was going to come into power on the earth, how are you going to protect the female from Satan? This is where the misunderstanding comes in religion. God wanted the man to pull the woman into the home. Not that the home is her place, the home is your base from which you grow and move out into the world. If Satan is going to dominate the world, then God wanted the woman in the house with a strong man as a protector. But what happened? Religion took that to an extreme. "Lock the woman down. Lock her up. Don't let her out into the world. Don't educate her. Don't teach and train her the Words of God."

In synagogues in the past, Jewish women could not learn the Torah like the men. In Islam, the women did not study the Qur'an like the men. And in Christianity also, women could not preach or teach because it was forbidden for a woman to do that up until recent times. Sisters, you're going to have to bear witness to the truth. In most societies on the earth, women are persecuted. Women are oppressed. America is the most enlightened society on earth, yet women in America are oppressed. You may say, "No, I'm not oppressed, I'm free." You are blind to the level of your own oppression. You think you're free but you're not free to be what God made you; you're free to be what man wants to make you.

You have become a piece of meat in this society. You are not a woman with spirit or intelligence to think and plan and create and be a balance for the man in government, politics, business, or religion. You are kept out of everything. By locking you out, man's own power has made him unbalanced. His own power has driven him crazy. He has made a world that is so wicked and self-destructive that, if you don't rise as a mother and a woman to take your place, the world will go down and take you down with it.

When you give power to a man, that power needs to be balanced. Power should always be balanced with the compassion, mercy, and tenderness that comes from the feminine side of human nature. When you keep women out of government, you keep compassion out of it. So, men have made war and more war to eat up

71

the lives of your children. You can say nothing because you have had no voice.

## The duty of men

This is America. You are a piece of meat. Who styles your clothes? What do they have in mind when they style your clothes? Who is advertising using your flesh on television? What do they have in mind when they take your clothes off and say, "I'm Ellen, fly me to the moon?" What do they have in mind, Sister, when they're selling mattresses and you have to lay on a mattress half-nude? What do they have in mind when they have to strip you to make you reveal your form so that men may see your form and never come to see you as you really are?

Today, if you think you have a good shape, you want to show it because, if you show it, you're going to get attention—but the wrong kind of attention. Some of you say a man ought to be able to control himself. He ought to be able to, but it is very difficult for a man to control himself and you are disrobed. Man was not made to exercise control in the presence of a naked woman. If a man exercises control in the face of a naked woman, you begin to wonder, what is it? You must help a man keep control. You must help a man keep control. If you don't help him, he'll be a dog for the rest of his life. You must help him to become a man.

You know that when you can control a man, you lose respect for him. You want someone you can look up to, not down at. If I start saying things that are false, let me know. But I haven't said anything false and I'm not going to say anything false because the Honorable Elijah Muhammad didn't teach me falsehoods. He taught us truth. Sisters, it is natural for you to test a man because you must know what you have. You devise little things to test him and see. Some of you are very, very, very surprised when you find he's not what you thought he was because you tested him.

The reason there is so much adultery among us is because we, as men, are not fulfilling our role as men. Someone must empower man again and show man his duty. That's why I am so grateful to Almighty God Allah for giving to us the Honorable Elijah Muhammad to show us what our role must be as a man. We must be providers. Any man who is not a provider is a man with whom you are going to lose patience.

Sister, if you must feed him and you're saying, "Honey, I'll buy you a suit. Baby, don't worry about nothing. You just go on home and keep everything together. I'll be home at 5. I'm working," and he's home waiting on you; and you have to bring the groceries home and pay the bills—after a while, what do you begin to think about him? You're looking at the man in your life like he is a child, and he starts calling you mama. "Hey, mama! How you're doing, mama?" You say, "Hell, I'm not your mama. I'm your wife. I don't want to be your mother. I want to be your wife. I married you so you could be my husband." What is a husband? He's a man that takes care of something that he doesn't own.

Look at what society has done to the Black man. Jobs are moving out the country to Third World countries. Your husbands are probably unlearned and unskilled. Look at these young women who are going to college. Who's in college with you, Sisters? It's mostly women. Men aren't in college. When you come out with your degree, who is your counterpart among the males that you can look to and look up to and walk with as an equal?

He doesn't know what you know. He doesn't understand what you understand. So, he's already behind. The only thing he has going for him is his physical strength and sex. But you're going to get tired of all of that if the man doesn't develop his mind. So here you are, at home, angry and upset. You aren't in any mood to console anyone. You need some consolation yourself. Sisters, Sisters, we have to break this cycle. We must start somewhere.

## An example: Khadijah Farrakhan

I thank God for His Coming and for giving to me personally a teacher that could help me become a man. Honestly Sisters, I could never have become a man if that man, the Honorable Elijah Muhammad, didn't teach my wife how to help me be a man. Stand up, Sister Farrakhan. I want you to come up here a minute. Come right on up. They say behind every great man, there's a woman. A lie. *Beside* every man and sometimes in front of every great man, there's a woman. Thank you for standing for her because she really deserves it.

The Honorable Elijah Muhammad taught her how to help me to become a man. I'm not going to let her say this, but she would tell you if I wasn't here, that I wasn't always the man that I am today. She would tell you I was a mess. She might say that. She learned how to control her mouth and how to use her mouth wisely because a man can't take being cut down by the woman that he loves. If you're cutting him down, what are you going to do with him after you cut him up? You might as well put him in the frying pan and eat him. Don't cut your man up. All Black men have the potential to be godly, powerful great men but you must know how to bring it out of them.

My wife doesn't suffer any abuse, not that kind. I hit her once. We've been married 40 years. I hit her once. Once. She hit me back and that was the end of that. This is true confession night. I felt so bad because she and I have known each other since she was eight years old, and I was 11 years old. In a couple of months, we will have been married 41 years, and my children have never seen their father strike their mother. They have hardly seen an argument between us. Whatever she has to say to me, she says it, but they don't hear it. Thank God. I hear it. That's important.

When you beat up your man in front of the children, you're cutting him down. He doesn't feel like he's a man anymore. His voice gets loud. Then, he grabs you in the throat. Before you know it, you're walking around the house. The children are devastated watching you all beat each other up. Sometimes if it's in the kitchen, you'll stab him. Or if it's in the bedroom, you'll shoot him. Most of the domestic violence is due to man and woman not knowing how to properly relate to each other in a time where there's so much stress on the man, on the woman, and on the children in a racist society.

Thank you, sweetheart (speaking to his wife as she returns to her seat in the audience). She has given me nine children. We have 25 or 26 grandchildren and one great-grandchild and many more on the way. So, I think, Sisters, I may be qualified to say a few things to you that will help you make his life and your life better.

## Domestic violence, incest, and rape

When a man starts getting loud, showing his authority, that's not the time to challenge him. That's like the policeman on the corner saying, "Alright, get off the corner," and you're going to say to him, "Man, I'm a taxpayer, you don't tell me..." He says, "Oh, yeah." Then, he reaches for the stick or gun because he has to show his authority because his authority was challenged. Your children are under your authority. When you raise your voice at them, what child do you have that can raise their voice back at you and still have teeth? My mother would not allow me to do something like this (sucking teeth). You suck your teeth, and you'll be looking for them. And you better not stomp off and slam doors. She'll come right behind you with a broom or something. You are in authority over your children and your authority demands respect.

The Bible says [1 Corinthians 11:3] Christ is the head of man, and man is the head of woman. To be a head, you must have a head. This presupposes that the male will have wisdom to rule his house. Even if he doesn't have the wisdom, he still feels he has authority. When he speaks and you give him a heavy word back, he must come back with one heavier. Before you know it, the voices rise decibel after decibel. He's being beaten in the argument because most of the time he can't win the argument. When you beat him in the argument, the only way he can win is to beat you with his fists. Who wins in that kind of situation? Nobody.

My wife was trained that, when I acted the fool, don't act it with me. She isn't a soldier for me to order around but sometimes I would give orders. I thought that I was a good F.O.I., a good Fruit of Islam. I'm giving orders to the men around the mosque, I should be able to come home and give some orders. She was very wise. She didn't respond. She waited until I calmed down, and said, "You know, such and such and so and so, and such and such and so and so. Do you understand?" Talking to me like that, she preserved my little budding manhood. She didn't crack it up because she could have cracked it up so easily. But if she cracks up my manhood, what is there for her to love after she destroys me. So, she's trying to build me into something that she can love. Isn't that beautiful?

Sisters, many of you are professional women. It's wonderful that you are lawyers, doctors, chemists, and businesspeople. But you are never going to be happy as a woman until you know how to make a home and make a man happy in your life.

Sisters, I don't care how much your law practice is successful. You have money. You have a BMW. You have a nice home. Many of you would trade all of that if you just had a good man that you could come home to. Sisters, when you get a man who is worth investing in, learn how to help cultivate him. If you're going to give children to that man, you want that man to stay around and help you rear your children. You don't want to run him out the house. You want to keep him coming home and working hard and bringing the money home. This is what you want.

Let's look at reality. Reality says the Black man today is in trouble. There's no work for him. He's not really interested in the type of education that's being offered. He's hanging on the corner. He's into drugs or gangs. He joins the army or he's in prison. What you have as a pool to pick from is little or nothing to make something of your life and his. This is reality now.

Many men do not know how to handle you. You're too strong. You're too Black. You're too powerful. When you beat him down, he goes out and he changes. Suddenly, a strong man becomes sweet. You have beautiful, handsome, strong Black men who have turned into women. You know there's not enough men around for you. When you go to find one, he's gone another way or he's in drugs or he's into crime or he joins the army or he's in prison. What are you to do? Many are turning in on themselves and women are becoming other than themselves because they can't find any fulfillment in a man. America is degenerating into a modern Sodom and Gomorrah, and nobody wants to talk about it. Nobody wants to address it.

Men are taking off their daughters. Very few women have escaped some form of incestual relations. That's sad. A man has a daughter from you who looks just like you looked when you were 16. Your daughter grows to love her father while you have grown accustomed to your husband. "He'll probably be home at 6. I'll leave his dinner on the stove, or he can get it himself."

But your daughter runs to the door to meet him. She says, "Daddy, you want something to eat?" She'll cook something for her father while you're in the room looking at television. He loves his daughter but now it grows into an unnatural kind of thing. He doesn't know how to take the beauty of her innocent love and adoration of him as a father.

Before you know it, he's having sex with his own child. He does not know what this is doing to your daughter. It is literally killing her as a female. If your father can't be any good, what man then can you trust if you can't trust your own flesh and blood father? What man can you trust if you can't trust your uncle? What man can you trust if you can't trust your grandfather?

When my wife was in the women's class of the Nation of Islam, she told me one day that Elijah Muhammad said that a man should not be left alone at home with his daughters. When she said that to me, I was highly insulted. I said I know he didn't say nothing like that; some crazy woman down there is trying to poison you. I was upset.

But when I became a minister and began to hear cases of incest, I knew and understood the reality. You don't want to talk about it because it's something that you put in the back of your mind and act like it never existed. But deep down inside, you are hurting. You can't really be to any man like you should because, if a father rips you off, there's very little left you can give.

This is why crimes against women should be punished severely. In the holy world, a man cannot rape a woman and live. In the Holy Land where you and I once lived, any man who rapes a woman is either stoned to death or beheaded. He is killed. That kind of law should be brought back because once a woman is raped, only God can bring her back to what she really should be. You don't realize your sacredness.

## Sex and the fruit of the womb

A woman should never be a free-for-all thing, for any man to just sleep with. A man ought to be worthy of you. If you don't put any value on yourself, then any man that you think has the right kind of story to tell or line to give, you will allow your own biological need to let a man make a fool out of you, then go and talk about you to his friends. Sisters, don't be angry with me. I'm just talking to you like I know the Honorable Elijah Muhammad and God would be pleased that I say these things because preachers are not talking like this. Teachers are not talking like this. Society is not thinking like this. Someone has to say these things and then try to live the kind of life that these words represent.

Sisters, this is not a putdown to you. This is not a putdown. You are too good to allow anybody the freedom to have you. You're just too good for that. Do you know why you do this? You don't think enough of yourself. You really think sex is not a big thing. Sisters, when you give yourself to someone, it ought to be because they have committed themselves to you, not just with their mouth. When you give yourself to a man, the issue that comes from that ultimately is an offspring. If that man has not made the right commitment, he walks away and leaves you with a baby. You can't find him to support his issue and you have died to give him life.

That's what birth is. The Honorable Elijah Muhammad said the pain of birth is equal to the pain of death. When the body shuts down in death, there is pain. The righteous want to die easy because death is painful. God takes the righteous away in a beautiful manner.

Birth is very painful. When you go through that pain for someone that you don't even love, how can you be to the child what you should be as a mother if you don't love the person whose seed you are carrying? Sisters, I'm getting deep into something, and I don't want you to feel any pangs of guilt. God is not here to condemn you but to uplift you. Anything that you have done wrong, God is here to forgive you, not judge you, but to offer you forgiveness.

This is what's wrong with religion. We, as preachers, are so doggone hypocritical to preach fire and brimstone on every sinner when we, ourselves, are guilty of some of the same things for which we condemn others. The scriptures of the Bible [Isaiah 64:6] teach the righteousness of man is as filthy rags in the sight of God. The Holy Qur'an teaches [Surah 16:61] that if God were to punish man for his sins, not one soul would be left alive on the earth. That includes the Pope, that includes the president, that includes the Minister—all of us have fallen short of the Glory of God and all of us stand in need of God's Mercy.

When I speak these things, I'm not speaking as a holy man. I'm trying to be a good man. I'm not speaking condemningly but hopefully to inspire you to a higher living. Sisters, look at what our children are doing. This is the most beautiful generation we've ever produced but they are living in the worst time that any nation has ever been since nations have been on the earth. Never was there a time when so much murder and destruction has been carried out by children. The jails are filled with young people. Many of them—10, 11, 12 years old—have killed other human beings. They are cold and heartless. They are your fruit. They come from your womb. What did we do to produce this generation?

Sisters, you have the right of choice. You have the right to choose to whom you will offer yourself. Once that act is consummated and life is forming in you, if you destroy the fruit of your womb, you are destroying the answer to your own prayers. My Sister over there is rocking a beautiful little baby. She may not know who that baby is, but God knows because Jesus looked just like that.

79

Jesus had a breast in his mouth, just like that. When you kill the fruit of your womb, the potential answer to cancer, lupus, sickle cell anemia, and all scientific questions is going to come from the womb of a woman. If you kill the fruit of your womb, you do not know who you may be destroying that could answer the critical problems of our time.

## An example: Sumayyah Farrakhan

My mother had very strange and extenuating circumstances surrounding her pregnancy with me. My father she married. He was a handsome man and a womanizer. My mother was a black, black woman, beautiful, strong, too much for him. He liked to play so she put him out of her life and met another man, but she was still married to my father. From the other man, she had a son, my older brother. Then my father, her first love, came back into the picture. You know how memories are—memories (He sings "memories"). In a moment of weakness, she had a relationship with her husband— she had not divorced him—and I was conceived. He goes away. She's pregnant, staying with another man, has a child from that man. Now she says, "Oh, my God! What am I going to do?" That's a problem, isn't it.

What's the first thought? "I have to get rid of this." In those days, they didn't have abortion clinics. In those days, you used a hanger. In those days, you had all those terrible things that women do to themselves and sometimes end up killing themselves as well as the child. She tried three times to abort me, but God didn't let it be. After the third time, this woman prayed. She was in trouble; she knew she was in trouble.

When you're in trouble, who do you have to go to? She went to God. "Lord, help me. Lord, help me." The more she prayed, all her supplications and prayers were going down into the womb. She was making me a man of God without ever knowing what she was making. It was uncertain circumstances. Some of you tonight who are pregnant and there are circumstances that you don't want to face, pray, Sister, and ask God for strength because you don't know what you may be killing.

My mother decided, "I'm going to have this baby." She hoped, "Lord, the first child was boy. I hope this is a girl. And I hope she's dark-skinned. Maybe if it's a girl and she's dark-skinned, I might be able to tell this Brother, 'She's just strange looking, that's all.'" Lo and behold, it wasn't a girl and it wasn't dark-skinned. The jig was up. She had to confess the truth. I caused the breakup of that relationship. She didn't want my father because he was a womanizer. She took my brother and me and left town and made a life without a man, like many of you are forced to make a life without a man.

If you don't have a man, remember God. My mother didn't know that the circumstances around which I was conceived in her womb would make me the man that I am today. She wanted a girl and she would make a child with the characteristics that represent the feminine side of the nature of God—mercy, compassion, forgiveness, and longsuffering. It takes that kind of person to redeem a people in our condition. If you don't have mercy and compassion and longsuffering and forgiveness, you'll be so bitter because your own people will become your worst enemies.

I am rejected of my own people, a certain class of them. But there is no Black man today who can call Black men and women and they respond. You didn't respond to the call of Farrakhan. You responded to the call of God Himself. It is God Who inspired you to come here tonight. You said you wasn't going but something moved inside you and you said, "I'm going. I want to hear this man for myself. I want to see just what Farrakhan is talking about. He's going to talk to all women. I want to know what Farrakhan has to say about women." Here you are.

## A woman's walk alone with God

Your womb is sacred. The circumstances that surround each pregnancy determines the quality of the person you're bringing forward if you know what to do when the child is in the womb. My mother wasn't taught what to do; circumstances made her pray. She was so insecure, she had to find refuge in God. She made me insecure as a child, but I never found my refuge in drugs, guns, or people. I have found my refuge in God. Because I made God my refuge, I stand today speaking to the government and to our oppressor, as a man without fear because, "Yea, though I walk through the valley of the shadow of death, I fear no evil because God is with me" [Psalm 23:4].

The reason you are here is because God is with you. This beautiful Sister just came down the aisle and sat down. Sister, I saw you while I was driving here. I saw you walking towards this place. As I drove past you, I said a prayer that God would bless me to say a word that would reach you. As I look at our women, you are so beautiful, but you are so in need of the right guidance for your life.

Sisters, in the Bible in Genesis, you see Eve alone. Adam is gone. Eve is alone. The serpent comes. If you look in the New Testament, you see Mary alone without any man by her side. In the Book of Revelation [12:5], you see a woman running in the wilderness about to deliver a man-child who is going to rule the nation with a rod of iron, but you don't see any man with her. In Genesis [16:7], Hagar is running in the wilderness out of Abraham's house—no man. But a woman who had to rear her child without a man—Mary—produced the greatest child that the world has known. What is that saying to you?

Even though Abraham had two sons, Ishmael and Isaac, and his covenant was with both, the one who was the child of the woman running in the wilderness was greater than the child who stayed at home. This is not an accident. God had His Hand in this, Sisters.

You are the children of slaves. Your man was destroyed, not by you but by the oppressor. Nobody has been able to rebuild the Black man. The government destroyed every leader that we produced who could represent a strong image to Black men. The government does not want a strong Black man among us. White men do not want you to fall in love with a strong Black man. Once you recognize a strong Black man, then they will never be able to bring forth from your womb children born to love the oppressor.

Sisters, this was by design. Most of you do not have a man by your side. You have children but no man by your side. Upon whom have you relied? You would have had to know God a lot more than your man has had to know God because you have children in a hostile world. You could not have brought us this far if you didn't have God walking with you and if you didn't try to walk with God. That's why the church is filled with women, and not too many men in the church—because you know you are the woman of God.

Now that God has been with you and the circumstances of your life have been so harsh, you have produced a generation unlike any generation but what you don't know is that you prepared your children for the Messiah. They're wild. They almost appear to you to be crazy. They're fearless. They're strong. They're cold. They're not listening to teachers and sometimes they're not listening to you. They are not listening if you are going to lead them back into the same pattern of the oppressor. Then, God is going to take your children away from you. That's why you must come up with a new way of thinking. A new mind must be put in you, Sister, so you can reconnect with your children.

**Empowering our children**

I am 61 years of age, but I can talk to your children and your children listen to Farrakhan. They are listening to something in Farrakhan. There is no age gap. Children are supposed to listen to their elders, but you are supposed to have something to tell them. If you are telling them the same old foolishness that we were told that made us slaves, children don't want to hear that. They don't want to hear you making excuses for this government and White people and the evil in their lives. They don't want you to do that.

Schoolteachers, they're not listening to you. It's not that you are bad, Teacher, but the method that you were taught doesn't work anymore. The psychology that you were given, it doesn't work anymore. Even the religion that you have been practicing, it doesn't work anymore because your religion was based on fear and ignorance. Your children are fearless, and they don't want you to try to make them afraid to make them right.

Religion used to frighten us—"the devil is going to get you and burn you" and "you had better get ready to die so you can go to heaven." Children learned some mathematics: If hell is under the ground and it is in the center of the earth, they know that the diameter of the earth is 7,926 miles. The radius is half of the diameter. So, the center of the earth would be half of 7,926 miles, which is 3,863 miles. If hell is 100 times hotter than the sun, which is 14,172 degrees hot; and a baby fell on the sidewalk in Arizona yesterday and the sun—93 million miles away—burned that child's skin; yet, hell is only 3,963 miles away, 100 times hotter than the sun, and you don't feel it on your feet—someone has been lying to you.

They told us that heaven was somewhere up in the sky and when you die, you're going to put on wings and you're going to fly away. Every person who dies and is buried in the ground, if you come back 10 or 20 years, they haven't moved anywhere. They have telescopes that can view stars and planets far away. They put a Hubble telescope in space so they can see as far as light years away in space. They haven't seen heaven yet. They told us heaven was up and so we're looking up. But the earth is turning, honey. What's up now, 12 hours later is down. So where is heaven?

Your children don't want foolishness anymore. You're not going to frighten them into believing in God. They already know there is a God, but they know that you don't know Him. How could you know God and be so poor, ragged, hungry, naked, out of doors, and ignorant at the same time?

Children will go to church with you when they're babies, and work with you and pray with you and tarry with you while you wait for the Holy Ghost to come. You say the Holy Ghost is going to give you power but it never gives you enough power to give them power to overcome the oppressor.

They begin to get tired of religion. They don't go to church anymore. They don't want to go to school anymore. They don't want to listen to you anymore. They don't want to hear the preacher anymore. They don't trust the politicians anymore. They're out in the streets, listening to one another rap. They're rapping to each other because they don't have a voice that is clear enough for them to hear.

That's why the oppressor is so angry with Farrakhan. He's a Black man who they don't control. He's a Black man who the children are beginning to listen to and he's not telling them about any pie in the sky stuff.

Heaven is right here on this earth. That's why you call it, "hereafter." Here after, not "there" after. Here after. Here on this earth, after the power of the wicked to rule is broken, the Kingdom of God will be established. Who's going to establish the Kingdom of God? Here is the Kingdom of God—it's these beautiful women.

## Onward and upward

No matter your color, no matter your race, if you are a woman, your womb is sacred. Your mind is sacred. Put something in your head more than just a soap opera and a TV drama and cheap novels. You must begin to feed your mind because, if you eat bad food, it corrupts your body. If you feed your mind filth, it corrupts your mind. They say a man is what he eats. As a woman thinketh, so is she.

If you're feeding your mind garbage, then you become a garbage pail. As a garbage pail, you can't produce nothing but maggots and flies. You're not a garbage pail so don't let anybody feed you garbage. Don't go to these shows and let a man get down funky and you're sitting there saying, "Go on baby, go on baby!" The more you allow it, the more they'll do it. Get up and walk out on the chump and demand your money back.

Make the man act better. Make him do right. Some of these men have become so filthy because you like it. They come out half-naked on stage. Some will take out their private parts on stage and

85

you say, "Oh, look at it!" You're encouraging this craziness. But if you, Sisters, turn from your wicked ways, you'll force a man to change because a nation can rise no higher than its woman. If we want to rise, then we must lift up our women. You must go to the pinnacle of knowledge, wisdom, and understanding.

Are you ready to travel? Onward and upward? From this night forward, Sisters, feed your mind knowledge, wisdom, and understanding. Feed your mind a higher knowledge so you can act on a higher plane and let no man pull you down.

## Embracing sisterhood

Sisters, in October, we will have our first international Saviours' Day in Ghana. We are hoping that as many of you who would like to visit the Motherland would take that trip with us. The President of Ghana has agreed to open the convention and be one of our hosts along with members of government and business. You are welcome, any of you who would like to go. All the details are in the *Final Call Newspaper.*

Sisters, we're going to have prayer. How many of you understood what you heard me say tonight? Sisters, how many of you believe that what you heard tonight is true and good for us as a people? Thank you. To my Christian Sisters, I want you to know that I'm a Christian, too. To be a Christian is only to be crystallized into oneness with God following the example of Jesus Christ. I'm also a Muslim. What is a Muslim? You are a Muslim, too. A Muslim is one who believes in submitting his or her will to do the Will of God. Aren't you desirous of doing God's Will? That's a Muslim.

So why should we argue about labels? Look under the label and see the principles that undergird it and let us never be religiously divided again. Those of you who are Baptist, those of you who are Methodist, those of you who are Episcopalian, those of you who are Catholic, those of you who are Jehovah's Witness, Church of God in Christ, AME, CME—these are just names. Underneath it, there's only one God and one Christ.

Why should the house be divided? We must come together as a family. Sisters, I am your Brother. Therefore, your children are my nieces and nephews. If there is no father in the house, then a brother who is your Brother should be able to help you with your children. I want to be a help and the brotherhood wants to be a help. That's why I'm going throughout America talking to Black men. I thank you, Sisters in Atlanta, for understanding that we are not trying to be discriminatory against men tonight nor were we discriminatory when we talked to men and left you home.

We are trying to organize a Million Man March on Washington. Sisters, you have been our leaders. We want to show you how much we appreciate you. So, we're asking you to let us now take the point. We want to go to Washington and present our case before the government. We have built this country. Our fathers' sweat and blood soaks the soil of America and foreign battlefields for a freedom that none of us enjoy. We deserve more than what America has given us. We ought to demand that, as men. We ought to go and demand that for our wives, mothers, grandmothers, aunties, and babies.

So, my family, since you are a family, all of you are Sisters— from this night on, I want you to begin to think that you should love for your Sister what you love for yourself. If you see your Sister with something that you want, don't want it for yourself to take it from her. Be happy that she has something good and thank God for that. Do not let envy and jealousy divide our house. When one of us is going up, that's all of us going up. We must learn to think like that.

Some of you feel you're very beautiful and some don't feel so beautiful at all. Those of you who think you're very beautiful, don't get arrogant with it and try to take what doesn't belong to you. Those who think you're not so pretty, real beauty has never been here (pointing to his face). Real beauty is here (pointing to his heart). As much time that you spend cultivating the outer self, let's spend a little more time cultivating the real person which is on the inside. Every one of you are beautiful to me and you are certainly beautiful to God.

From this night on, when you see your Sister and she's down, don't walk past her. Help her up. If you can say an encouraging word to the prostitute, don't down the prostitute. Don't down her, don't down her. She's sometimes a better woman than most churchgoers because she's less hypocritical. When you see your Sister is a prostitute, help her to see the beauty of herself. Remember Mary Magdalene. She was, some say, a woman of ill repute. When all the disciples ran out on Jesus, his mother Mary was there, and Mary Magdalene was also there. So don't talk down to the less fortunate. That's your Sister. Help lift her up.

After I say the prayer, would you please turn to one another and embrace each other. It will take but a few minutes. Just embrace one another. Go past the ones that you know and embrace someone you don't know. Just be sisterly.

## Minister Farrakhan's honor and gratitude

When you go out into the night, I hope maybe they'll ask you, "What did Farrakhan say?" You tell them that you met your Brother. He didn't teach you to hate anyone. Did he? Do I sound like a hater to you? That's because I'm not. If they say, did he say anything anti-Semitic? Tell them no, he just spoke truth. It would be unthinkable that, with our problems, I would come in here to try to get you to hate White people or Jewish people or any other people. That is silly and it is unworthy of me. If 400 years of evil has not made you hate someone, it's impossible for anyone to teach you to hate. Sisters, let's have prayer.

To all my sisters from New York and Boston that I know and have seen you again but I'm not able to touch you, please—my wife is here, she knows where I'm staying. I want to see you. I want to touch you. I want to thank you personally for the help that you gave me. I couldn't be what I am if it were not for you all.

Wherever I go and however God lifts me, I want you all to know—you, Muslims who built the Nation of Islam under the guidance of the Honorable Elijah Muhammad—that you all are the wind beneath my wings. Wherever I go, I will carry you always with me in my heart.

Marlene Shah, my Sister, I want to see you. Sister Susie, all your daughters, I want to see you. You saw me when I came in the Nation. You all saw me. Sister Ruth, you saw me when I came in and watched me grow up. I just want to see you. Sister Rosetta, I must see you, please. May Allah (God) bless all of you. All of you who I don't get a chance to see, you have honored me beyond words.

## Hope and prayer

As Sister Tynnetta Muhammad or Sister Ava Muhammad said, I don't think anything has ever taken place like this in America. I'm going to do this in many other cities, but we have to pull our women together and give you a push.

Don't lose hope in the Black man. He's going to be alright. Just let me get to him with the words of the Honorable Elijah Muhammad. You just help him. When you go home tonight, encourage him. Be kind to him. He's beat down by everybody. Don't you do it, even if he acts a fool. Go in a room, suck it up, and get it together. Come on out and say, "Oh well, honey…"

A Sister has a song she'd like to dedicate before prayer. (speaking to Sister Donna Farrakhan: Oh, she didn't sing it yet? You all should have sung that before we started, honey.) This is my daughter, one of them. This is my wife's twin. Sisters, we should have all sang, "Lift Every Voice and Sing" before we started because it isn't right for us to start anything without that. So, if you don't mind, before prayer, can she sing one verse of it? Let's stand for the Black National Anthem. (The Sister sings.)

Let us march on til victory is won. A new day for us has begun, Sisters. May God bless each and every one of you. May every word that He guided me to speak go into your heart and soul, remain with you, and let it make a change in your life for the better.

With your heads slightly bowed, kindly follow us in our closing prayer. I will pray a part of it in Arabic and a part in English.

*Bismi l-lāhi r-raḥmāni r-raḥīm*
*alḥamdu lil-lāhi rab-bi l-'ālamīn*
*ar-raḥmāni r-raḥīm*
*Māliki yawmi d-dīn*
*iy-yāka na'budu wa'iy-yāka nasta'īn*
*ihdinā ṣ-ṣirāṭa l-mustaqīm*
*Ṣirāṭa l-ladhīna 'an'amta 'alayhim,*
*ghayri l-maghḍūbi 'alayhim*
*wala ḍ-ḍāl-līn*

*In The Name of Allah, The Beneficent, The Merciful.*
*Praise be to Allah, the Lord of the worlds,*
*The Beneficent, The Merciful.*
*Master of the Day of Judgment.*
*Thee alone do we worship, Thine aid we seek.*
*Guide us on the right path,*
*the path of those upon whom You have bestowed favors,*
*not the path of those upon whom Your wrath is brought down,*
*nor of those who go astray.*

*O Allah, we thank you for this beautiful evening and for each and every one who has attended. We pray, O Allah, that you will help us lift the burden of grief and suffering from the hearts of our women that they may be inspired to know that they are second only to You. Only when man respects and honors women, can men truly be said to respect and honor God. A nation can rise no higher than its women. So, we beg you, O Allah, to pull our women up from the mud of civilization where the wicked have placed them and place them on top of civilization so that we, as a nation, can rise because they as women have risen up.*

*This is the Resurrection, and this is the Ascension of our women to the Right Hand of God. Help them to move speedily and quickly toward You. Oh Allah, we ask that you go with them to their places of abode and guide them and feed them that they may feed the young, that we may*

*make a difference in this world. We ask all of this in the name of your servant, the Honorable Elijah Muhammad. For I bear witness there is no God but Thee and I bear witness that Muhammad is Your Messenger.*
*Amen.*

Sisters, thank all the M.G.T. and G.C.C. from Mosque No. 15 in Atlanta and all the Sisters who came to help make this night possible. Thanks to the F.O.I. for passing out the flyers. Thanks to all of you for coming. Don't leave until you hug your Sister and tell her you love her. May Allah (God) bless you as I greet you in peace. *As-Salaam Alaikum!*

# 5 SISTA TO SISTER: THE VALUE OF THE FEMALE

Thank you, Reverend [Maxine] Walker.

In The Name of Almighty God Whom we refer to as Allah, The Beneficent, The Merciful. We give Him praise and thanks for His Mercy and Goodness to the human family that whenever any member of that family strays from His path and loses His Divine Favor before He punishes, He always raises from among that people a prophet or a messenger to whom He gives what is called divine revelation or scripture.

We thank Him for Moses and the Torah or the Old Testament. We thank Him for Jesus and the Gospel. We thank Him for Muhammad and the Qur'an. Peace be upon these worthy servants of almighty God Allah.

I am a student of the Most Honorable Elijah Muhammad and what I will share with you tonight is from His teaching to me which embraces the Torah, the Gospel, the Qur'an, all three books of God that represent three members of the monotheistic family of Abraham: Jews, Christians, and Muslims.

Unfortunately, the family is divided. Unfortunately, Satan has put hatred among the members of a family which Abraham would be hurt over and God is certainly displeased. If we could unite Muslims, Christians and Jews who believe in the oneness of God, who believe in Jesus the Messiah. who believe in all the scriptures brought by the prophets of God, we could defeat Satan and the Kingdom would be right here on this earth with us.

I greet all of you, my dear Brothers and Sisters, with the greeting words of peace, *As-Salaam Alaikum*. To the apostle whose house we are honored to be in, to the members of the clergy that serve here, to the members of the clergy who are present tonight, to Reverend Maxine Walker whom we honor this evening, and to all the Brothers and Sisters who are present, I'm very, very honored to have this opportunity to share a few words with you.

Reverend Maxine Walker has been a very dear friend of mine for the last maybe 25 years. I have always wanted to form a bond, a relationship with the Christian community and Christian clergy because I think we misunderstand each other. By not dialoguing with each other, Satan makes us think we are all different when, in reality, the root of all of us is the same.

Through the good office of Reverend Maxine Walker, she was instrumental in bringing several hundred ministers over a period of time that we could meet, converse, dialogue, and ask each other questions. In a spirit of love and brotherhood, we made great connections. Without those connections, the Million Man March would not have been a reality. Without Christian unity and our love for each other, the Million Man March would not have been.

So, I'm honored to be here tonight to share words, but also to pray to Almighty God that He will give time and more life to our Sister that she may continue to do the good work that she does, which is bringing people together.

## Our Father Who art in heaven

The theme of her many meetings like this is "Sista to Sister." I failed to ask Reverend Walker what she was thinking when she gave this event that title. Since I didn't ask her and didn't get her answer, I began to think on it myself. I saw a lot in the title "Sista to Sister." *Sista* seems to be ebonic, which sort of represents a Black woman who is not quite what she should be. *Sister* is different from *sista*, but sista is moving to or toward becoming sister. How could you be a sister if you didn't recognize a common father?

Apostle [Maxine Walker] says the Kingdom has come [the event slogan] but that's part of a prayer when the disciples asked Jesus, "Teach us how to pray." Jesus said, "Pray on this wise: Our Father." Sista lost her connection to the Father, but sister has a connection to the Father. The sista who has lost her way is moving toward her sister who's reintroducing her to the Father. Until we recognize the Father, we cannot consider ourselves Sisters or Brothers because it is the Father who makes us Brother, Sister and family. That brings us to the value of a woman.

This is a world that does not value the female. She's looked upon more like a plaything than the serious creation that Almighty God intended for her to be. The sad thing about sista is she doesn't recognize her value. So, she plays into Satan's game of degenerating the female and seeing herself only as an object of pleasure. The enemy undresses her, because the enemy wants her to use the beauty of her form to attract the natural lust in a man, to keep his mind focused below the navel in the underworld so he can never see the value of her and climb to the heavenly part of his natural existence.

The moment you lower a woman, you automatically lower the man. The moment you elevate the woman, you elevate the man. How is that so? My teacher, the Honorable Elijah Muhammad said where there are no decent women, there are no decent men, for the woman—the black woman in particular—is the Mother of Civilization. I would like to take a journey with you to help sista see the value of being a Sister as a child of God.

## The glory of God

In the beginning when God created the heavens and the earth, He did five days of magnificent work. On the sixth day He created a man. The Bible says that there was no tiller of the ground. So, God evidently created the man to do some heavy work. Tilling the ground is an act of cultivation. Everything that God created was already here, but He wanted to make a man as not *a* glory of God but *the* glory of God. This is very powerful to attempt to understand.

The sun is a glory. The moon is a glory. The mountains, the seas, the rivers, the lakes, the birds, the bees, the fowl, the fish— these are glories of God, and they glorify God. But **The** Glory of God. The definite article when it is used sets that thing apart from everything else that is "a" because this is "the." The Bible didn't give that position, "the glory," to man alone.

In that act of creation, if you study the scripture carefully, there were two people made at the same time: "Male and female created he them [and blessed them] and called their name Adam" [Genesis 5:2]. Adam is not a man. Adam represents the beginning of the human community. The Qur'an says it a little differently but it's a very beautiful scripture: "Keep your duty to Allah as it ought to be kept" [Surah 3:102]. He created you from a single essence and from that same essence created his mate" [Surah 4:1; Surah 7:189].

If that single essence is God Himself, which it is, then male and female are direct descendants of the Creator. You're not just somebody. You are direct descendants of Him Who originated the heavens and the earth. You are not Black because you are cursed. You're Black because you are the original creation of the Creator. This is not racism. This is actual facts. Two Caucasian people cannot produce a Yellow man, much less a Brown man, not to think of a Black man.

The Bible says [Acts 17:26]: "He has made from one blood all nations." Blood is the life fluid of some creature. That creature, the Honorable Elijah Muhammad said, is the original man. The first man that God created is a Black man. That's why anthropologists search for the origin of man in Africa, not Europe. They keep going back to Africa, finding bones older and older and older of Black men.

They call the first woman "Eve." When *Newsweek* magazine wanted to depict Adam, they depicted him as a man of color. They depicted Eve, the mother of all humanity, as a Black woman. The world knows this, so you shouldn't be ashamed to claim who you are:

Sister. You are a direct descendant of God Himself. In you is Him. His essence is a part of the male and the female.

As Satan caused the fall of Adam, he has caused the fall of male and female. We are no longer what God intended for us to be. He created man and woman in His image and after His likeness and gave the man and woman power and dominion. We're not exercising that right now because we are not what He created us to be. We have fallen from the high level in which the Creator created us, and we are on the level of the beasts of the field. How did we fall like this? Satan interfered with our relationship with our Creator.

Brothers and Sisters, it's wonderful to sing glorious songs of praise. It's wonderful to preach words of praise. But Jesus didn't come into this world for us only to sing words of praise or preach words of praise. He came to bring us back to our original position with God, as a god ourselves. You say, "What? Now, Farrakhan, I think you're stretching things a little bit." No, no, no. No.

David the Psalmist said [Psalm 82:6], "Ye are gods; and all of you are children of The Most High." If you are a god and I am a god and she is a God, and we are gods from *The* God, then Satan's job is to disconnect the children from the Father so that the wisdom, power, and spirit of the Father won't be seen in His children.

Look at the condition of our people, and what we're doing to ourselves and what we're doing to one another. Regardless to our songs of praise, we act contrary to what we sing about. We act contrary to what we preach about. Pardon the expression, I don't mean to hurt any feelings, so I'll start with ourselves—*we* are hypocritical to what we say because we are not living the life that brings the Kingdom into reality. Sista to Sister.

## Reflecting God

Jesus came into the world for a very special purpose from our vantage point and I think it's your vantage too. Man had fallen so low and far from himself that he needed a redeemer. He needed a saviour. He needed someone to reconnect fallen humanity back to

God so that we could once again reflect God. The people walked in darkness, gross darkness the people but upon them hath the light shined [Isaiah 9:2].

My dear Sisters, we can't teach a subject like this unless we understand what the slave master's vision was when he brought our fathers across the Atlantic Ocean to be made slaves. He never intended for us to reflect the Creator. He wanted to take the place of our Father and become our master. When you beat fear into a people and make them call you "massa," they are afraid to disobey you. Then you can shape and mold them in the way you want them to be. You can't blame the clay; you must look at the potter.

Who made us into this grotesque being that we have become that we are now the number one killers of ourselves, destroyers of each other, disrespecting our women and disrespecting our mothers? Most of my Sisters in here have children but very few have a good family life where there's a male, a female, and children. You are in this thing almost by yourself. Nature brings male and female together. Nature makes us procreate. If the man runs away from his responsibility, you are left alone with the burden of rearing your children but robbed of the knowledge of how to do it.

The Bible says [Proverbs 22:6], "Train up a child in the way he should go: and when he is old, he will not depart from it." What is the way that the child should go? How can you train the child up in that way if you're not sure that you know the way?

It was not the slave master's desire that you should know how to train your children in the way that they should go. He wanted us to train the children to be better tools of service for his purposes. As a result, the Black male had to be destroyed and the Black female had to be remade to bring into this world children that would look up to, follow, and almost worship the slave master and his children. That's a fact.

Religion has been helpful to us. But the enemy has taken our love for Jesus Christ and turned us into subtle worshippers of himself. He painted the Lord in his image. We don't have any problem if Jesus is Caucasian. We don't care about that. We know he's one that we should follow and submit to regardless of color. But Jesus happened to be Black. This is not just me saying this, he said it.

Jesus said [Revelation 22:16], "I am the root and offspring of David, the bright and the morning star." David's father was Jesse [Isaiah 11:1, There shall come forth a rod from the stem of Jesse, and a branch shall grow out of its roots]. David's son was Solomon. Solomon said [Solomon 1:5], "I am black, but comely, O ye daughters of Jerusalem." If he was Black, his daddy could not have been something else.

Jesus had hair like lamb's wool and feet like burnished brass. His mother Mary was an Egyptian. Egypt is in Africa. Even though Jesus taught in Palestine, she took her baby and fled to Egypt that the scripture might be fulfilled: "out of Egypt I have called my son" [Matthew 2:15; Hosea 11:1]. Sista has been ruined. It takes the Coming of God and the re-introduction to His Christ that will bring us back to where God wanted us to be.

**The Kingdom of God within**

Let's go back 2,000 years a moment. In all the movies of Jesus, they include his mother Mary, Martha, and another Mary. How were those women dressed around Jesus? Did you see any with a miniskirt? You didn't see any of those sisters wearing hot pants? Why? Jesus knew the value of a female and he knew he couldn't build the Kingdom with naked women. Men can't think to build a Kingdom if they are looking at your finery, sista.

We want to move sista to Sister, a child of God. I don't want to say this in a way that makes you think I'm talking down to you because I am in love with you. When you love your people, you want to see your people better than what the enemy made of them. You want them made again in the image and the likeness of God.

Paul said [Romans 12:2], "Be not conformed to this world: but be ye transformed by the renewing of your mind." Why must your mind be renewed? Our minds were made by the slave master and his children into this grotesque shape. If you really study our people, we're beautiful on the inside, if you can get there. You must be a miner to mine out the good in us. Hell is at the surface and heaven is deep down. That's why Jesus said, [Luke 17:21], "the Kingdom of God is within you."

Why is there so much hell everywhere if the Kingdom is in us? It takes the spirit of a redeemer to be patient with our people to teach them and bring them up from the condition that they're in, to the condition that God wants. God wants to make our women the mothers of that Kingdom. That Kingdom cannot come through men; it comes through women.

It was women around Jesus at the end. The disciples ran away, except John. Peter said, "I don't know that man. I have never seen that man before." You know how Negros are. They're in love with you until the enemy comes. When the enemy gets a hold of a righteous man, speaks evil of him, and brings him before their courts of law, all you have to do is indict a Black person and the rest of them fly. "Child, did you get the news tonight? So-and-so was indicted." That's just a charge. It doesn't mean that they're guilty. All the enemy has to do is indict us, and we run from one another. They indicted Jesus. They charged a good man because he was bringing in a Kingdom that was not of this world.

How could we praise the Kingdom with one foot in the world? "C'mon, baby, let's get down. Shake it up, baby." Talking to your little girl. What are you making? The enemy has made it hard for the Redeemer. You say he paid the price for us. He did. He did. But don't think he paid the price, and we can still act a fool and won't get punished for it.

He paid the price and opened the way for us to go back to our original position with God in His image, His likeness, His khalifah in Arabic, which means "one who stands in the place of God." Jesus stands in the place of God. He said, "where I am, you may be also." That doesn't mean he's flying away and we are going to get up there. It means that he's on a plane at the right hand of Him

Who has wisdom and power over everything. He's calling us to our place beside him.

## What nature demands

Family, the Qur'an says [Surah 4:1], "Keep your duty to Allah, by Whom you demand one of another your rights." Did you know that the female has rights over the male and her nature makes a demand on him? Even if you don't know your nature, your nature is driving you to make a demand on any man who comes into your life. Do you know why he's running from you? The demand is so strong and he's so weak that your demand crushes him.

What is your demand? The Qur'an says [Surah 4:34], "men are the protectors and the maintainers of women." This is what God has set forth. Look at the order that Paul mentions [1 Corinthians 11:3] and how that order has been interfered with. It's God, Christ, man, woman, child. That's the order. God first, then Christ, man, woman, child. That's the order. The worse thing that Satan has done is interfere with the divine order. There's no woman looking to a man because the man is not looking to God.

How can we demand something from a woman when God is not making a demand on us that we're willing to obey. When you get caught up with a man, sista—and most of you got caught up with somebody—maybe he's good. I know he has the potential for sure. But you got caught up with him but didn't understand your nature. When a man tills the ground, that's why God brought him here. God brought him here to work hard to be a producer. When a man is a producer, working hard tilling the ground, bringing something up out of it that he can maintain his wife, protect her, and feed his family, a woman loves a man like that.

Sister, you're working hard today because the man doesn't have a job. If he has one, he's making less than you. Then, all of a sudden, your voice in the house is bigger than his. The order has been interfered with. God, Christ, man, woman—no, it's now God, Christ, woman, and maybe a man somewhere in that equation.

The Bible says [Isaiah 3:12], "Children are their oppressors and women rule over them." Satan has destroyed the order. Read Willie Lynch, a slave master on the island of Jamaica, and what he did. He broke the man in the presence of the woman. He put fear in the woman for his evil against her man and made the woman so protective of her male children, that she made them weak and her females strong.

You have girls who are strong and boys who are weak. Your love for your male child, particularly in the South, when that boy showed some "get up," you said, "Get up! Get on up North. You have an uncle in Chicago. Go on up there, boy, because if you stay down here you will get killed and you will get us killed. Get out of here." So, he didn't feel like he should challenge the enemy.

For his own safety, you protected him. You protected him from the wrath that you knew was in the slave masters' children, but it made him weak to challenge him. Today it's you, Black woman, on the battlefield and the man is waiting to walk behind you. That's why you can't honor a man. That's why you can't respect the man. He's not your protector. He's not your maintainer. He has been destroyed by the enemy. That's why Christ needs to be real in your life. Don't just talk about him. If he's real in your life, you become a man—a real man, not a punk man. When you become a real man, you start becoming an image of God. The woman then wants to console you. She wants to comfort you. That's her nature. When a man tilled the ground, he was worthy to be consoled.

This beautiful little girl, the daughter of our pastor. The beauty of her leaning on her father and the tender love that she has for dad, you grow up like that—innocent and beautiful, leaning on the breast up the male guide, protector, and maintainer in your house. That pastor, father of that precious daughter wants the right man for that child. He worries like I worry: "Lord, what kind of man will come into my child's life?" He and I, and we as men, must get busy making men for God so that she will never walk in the path of those who walked before her.

A man has a demand on you. If a man works hard and he's a protector and maintainer, what does he expect? He doesn't expect television to console him. He doesn't expect the music box to console him. No, his consolation is in you. When you are happy with a man—brothers, brothers, brothers, when she is happy with us! You don't have to ask a girlfriend to cook something for you. But today, she doesn't know how to cook, poor thing. She runs to the freezer, gets something made in a strange kitchen, pops it in the microwave, and kills you. But grandma? Go back and look at grandma and grandpa in the South.

That man was out tilling the ground. That man was out working hard. When he was coming home, he could smell the biscuits 50 yards from the house. He knew his wife was cooking. "Come on in, baby. How do you feel, honey?" He was so happy to get home because she made a home for him. She consoled him with the meal that she cooked. She consoled him with the touch of her hand. She consoled him with the warmth of her breast. She consoled that man. That's your nature.

But a man must be worthy of that. A man who is doing nothing deserves nothing. Here's a man who wants comfort from you, but he isn't doing anything for you. You want to give him nothing because he hasn't earned anything. After a while, love becomes painful. Sista! We must move toward being sister.

## A direct connection to God

I want to describe the woman of God for you. The woman of God doesn't get her blessings necessarily through a man, although that would be nice. Because the world is so messed up, the woman has to find a direct relationship with God. Men, if they were naturally in their right order, they would be wonderful spiritual teachers in their home. The woman could look to her husband as a teacher and guide. Poor fella today, poor us. Sister is going to college. Brother is in the street. Sister is becoming a doctor, lawyer, and engineer. Brother is singing songs. Brother is in prison. Brother is selling drugs.

She has no future. We are destroyed as a people, and we need God in our lives.

In conclusion, Hager was the handmaiden of Sarah in the Bible. Sarah was old and she couldn't bear children at that time. So, Abraham, the friend of God, went into Hagar and she conceived a child. At some point Sarah, though old, became pregnant. Now, that's a house where there is drama, heavy drama. Evidently something happened in the house. A woman doesn't like competition. In that part of the world, polygamy is the way of life but a woman who consoles a man doesn't want another woman consoling that man.

There's an awful lot of pain in our women because in their lives, there's not the kind of man who satisfies the soul. So, our women, in pain, eat and eat and eat. They become more and more obese, not because they want to be but they're hurting. They don't care. they're not living for themselves. They don't feel that a man is paying attention to them. Young girls dress in a way to get attention from men, not good attention but low-down attention. But it's attention. When you give birth to children and start losing your form, you may begin not to care for yourself. There's no man who is really paying attention to you, so you feel, "The heck with it. I'll just keep on eating. So what if I'm fat. So what if I'm out of shape. I'm not trying to attract anybody anyway." That's the wrong attitude. You should live for God and for yourself. You don't live for a man. You live for God, and you live for yourself. If there is a good man in your life, you can share the good of your life with him.

Sisters, Hagar was put out of Abraham's house. She's running in the wilderness with a baby while a man that's a prophet and the friend of God is in the house. Food is in the house but the woman who gave him a child is running in the wilderness without any food, looking to the hills for help. David the Psalmist said [Psalm 121:1], "I will lift up my eyes unto the hills." I think there should be a period there, and then the question is asked [Psalm 121-1-2], "from whence cometh my help? My help cometh from the Lord."

Hagar had a direct connection to God because in that wilderness He fed her, not Abraham. So she then could talk to Abraham as a man: "I know God, too. I didn't have to get Him through you. I got Him in the wilderness. In my pain, hunger and hurt, God came to me."

Every one of you sisters who don't have a man but have a connection to God, you have it all if you know what you have. If you have a connection to Him Who gave you life, then out of His Grace, He will give you a man. Don't look for one. Look for God in your life and the right man will come along. Just ask God to give you the spirit of discernment.

Family, if you look at our women, we are like Hagar running in the wilderness with our children looking to the hills for help. That's why in church, the strongest members are women. They're trying to find that connection to God through Jesus Christ.

## The center of our families

I was in a beautiful Baptist church in Houston, and I was talking about women. I mentioned Mary, the mother of Jesus. I said to a brother, would you honor your mother and honor the mother of Jesus if she came in the church? Would you allow her to come up and speak from the rostrum to the people? He said no, she would have to stand down there. I said, but brother, she gave you your savior. Isn't she worthy to give you a message? She's a holy woman. She was a woman who didn't know sin. She can't talk to a house full of sinners?

We have messed up religion. We have literally dishonored God by dishonoring the female. I appeal to us as men, don't be afraid of an intelligent woman. Be happy that you have an intelligent woman to be your helpmeet. Not a piece of meat, but a helpmeet to help you meet the obligation that God put on us as men, to be cultivators, producers, and rulers. A woman by your side when you want to help Christ build the Kingdom, she's your helpmeet in that noble idea. But if you are not a Kingdom builder, if you just want to feel good without doing good, then you will have lots of trouble in your home because a woman cannot abide a man who is nonproductive. Sisters who take care of men, **sisters who take care of men**, you spoil a man. Any woman who takes care of a man, he's your child. Therefore, you can't honor him in the role that God wants him to play when you've made him your child.

That's why he tells the fellows, "Come on over to my crib." His language tells you where his head is: "My house is a playpen. There's nothing productive going on there. It's my crib and I have some toys. When my woman has some serious business to do, she puts the pacifier in my mouth. I'm happy as I could be." You spoil him and you can't love him because your nature won't let you love what can't maintain you, can't protect you, and can't be a doorway for you to Jesus Christ.

You bring strange men in your house, and you have fine-looking young daughters. At nine years old, their bosom is bigger than yours. You think that man is looking at you. Sister, too many of our women have been spoiled by uncles, fathers, grandfathers, brothers, and cousins. When you spoil a woman, that pain lives until the Redeemer can take it away from her. She can't be made whole after being done like that, until God can come into her life and take that away from her.

Women, you are the natural protectors of your children. You must rise to your job. Protect your babies, particularly in a world like this. Your boys are smart as they can be from age one to five. You send them to school and suddenly you see them slipping backward. The educational system of the slave master and his children is a killing field.

That's why I'm happy for the apostle and the Kingdom School that he set up. Without God in your life and God in the center of your children's life, what do you have?

## Striving

Sisters, I hope that we'll move from sista to sister, recognizing God as our Father and that's what makes you my Sister. I want to be a good Brother to my Sister. When I met Reverend Maxine Walker, I met my Sister. She recognized me even though my religious name was Muslim. She looked all the way past that and she saw in me her Brother. I see Reverend Mitty Collier in the back. That's my Sister.

All the pastors, I love you all with all my heart because I know you have the power to change the reality of human life by good preaching of the Gospel and doing everything in your power to live that life. We're human and filled with frailties and weaknesses. We should not preach as though we are perfect. We should preach as though we are striving like they are. Once you set yourself up as being perfect and then they find a spot or blemish—like Senator [Larry] Craig saying, "I am not gay. I don't do those things."—they are killing and crucifying that man.

We, in leadership, should strive to be the best examples that we could be. Ask God's forgiveness for our shortcomings. But in the Christ—you call him "Christ" and that's his title. His name is Jesus. In the Qur'an, we see Jesus as the Messiah, as the Presence of God among human beings. We don't see him as an unattainable object. We see him as an example for us, so we try to rise to be like him.

I strive to be like him. That's why I'm hated. If you're not hated, check yourself because the Master was hated, and he said his disciples would be hated for his name's sake. They don't write bad about anybody like they write about me.

It's alright with me because greater is he that is in me than he that is in the world. They can't destroy the God that is within me. He's making a man out of me. I challenge government because I know God. I'm not someone trying to find Him. I know He is my backup. I know He is my strength. Like the Psalmist, The Lord is my strength, and He is my salvation, of whom then shall I be afraid? [Psalm 27:1].

Get up like a man of God and preach this Gospel without fear. Let God uphold you. He can't uphold you doing nothing. Challenge the world and let's bring in the Kingdom. This world is not worthy of us. Let's bring in the Kingdom.

When they send for you to send your children to die in Iraq, tell them, "Not my child." Stand up. "Not my child." I'll go to the draft board: "Not my sons. You won't take one of them to send them to die in your wickedness. I'm a Kingdom man."

If that frightens you, then you are not a Kingdom woman. You are still sista. May God bless us. Thank you for listening. Thank you. *As Salaam Alaikum.*

# 6 THE IMMEASURABLE, LIMITLESS VALUE AND BEAUTY OF THE WOMAN

In The Name of Allah, The Beneficent, The Merciful. We give Him praise and thanks for His Goodness and His Mercy to the human family that whenever any member of the family strays from His straight path before He punishes, He always extends His Mercy by raising up a prophet or a messenger from among that people. We are taught in the Holy Qur'an that every nation has received a messenger. The Qur'an names some but there are many that are not named. The ones that are named are important as they are guides to the last messenger. We thank Allah (God) for Musa or Moses and the Torah. We thank Allah (God) for Jesus and the Gospel. We thank Allah for Muhammad and the Qur'an. Peace be upon these worthy servants of Allah (God).

I am a student of the Honorable Elijah Muhammad whom I believe Allah (God) raised up for us. America, the most wicked of the nations of the earth, has never had a divine warner from Allah (God). As it was His pattern in the past, He always raised His warners and messengers from among the worst of the people—the people despised, the people rejected, the people oppressed, the people enslaved, the people exploited. His pattern is the same. it is just that we find it difficult to see that Allah's (God's) Mercy has extended to the Black man and woman of America who have been destroyed in our 450-year sojourn in America. A Black president has not changed our condition. I thank Allah (God) for His intervention in our affairs.

We believe that the Mahdi Who was prophesied to come is present and that His Power to set down every tyrant and set justice in the earth will be seen first and foremost in the United States of America. I thank Him for His Coming in the spirit and power of Allah (God). No man can set justice in the earth except God empower him to do that. No human being has that kind of power to set down every tyrant that is on this earth except he is empowered and anointed by God to do this kind of work. We believe that that Man has appeared among us.

He has weighed and measured the earth and the waters. He has pointed out to us the end of this world's time and that Allah, The Supreme, The Originator, The One God Who has no associates or partners, has declared the end of this world. He and He alone will bring it about. All of you should be tired of a world of so much evil and so much injustice. All of you, whether you are Christian or Muslim or Jew or even an agnostic or an atheist, should be tired of a world like this that we live in and should be praying that God would end this world and bring in something new, something better, that is called the Hereafter.

I'm not feeling too well today but when Master Fard Muhammad was among us, He came to Elijah Muhammad's home and asked him, "How did things go at the meeting today?" He [Elijah Muhammad] said, "I didn't go. I wasn't feeling well." He said, "Brother, when you have an assignment, you don't let sickness stop you. Go and die on your post." Too many of us make excuses to forsake an assignment.

There is no greater assignment than for God to call you and me "Muslims" and give us an assignment that was not fulfilled during the time of our holy Prophet Muhammad, peace be upon him (PBUH). He finished the course that Allah (God) had given him. He had four rightly guided caliphs who carried the word of the Qur'an and others after them into the known world.

Yet, hypocrites came in among the believers and turned the course of Islam. Now, we are no longer what Allah (God) and Prophet Muhammad (PBUH) wanted us to be. We are nationalists. We are Egyptians. We are Iranians. We are Iraqis. We are Jordanians. But there was no nation but the Nation of Islam that Prophet Muhammad set up. No other nation!

All these so-called Muslim nations are deviations. We must come back to the right path of God or suffer the chastisement of Allah (God) which is already in the Middle East and soon will be all over our planet. Allah (God) is sick of us making mockery of Him, saying prayers that don't mean anything, bowing down to the force of evil that runs this country, and wanting to make friends with Satan rather than becoming a favored friend of God.

**The foundation laid by women**

The enemy calls today "Mother's Day." I don't know how many billions of dollars the enemy has made commercializing on our natural love for our mothers. In Islam, every day is a day to honor our mothers. But the commercial nature of the enemy is to make money. On Jesus, we call it Christmas. Make money on his resurrection—they call it Easter. Make money on your girlfriend and boyfriend—it's Valentine's Day.

Make money on everything that they can think of to suck the blood out of the common people who are ignorant. Their ignorance is taken advantage of by a smart, crooked deceiver. I thank Allah (God) for all the mothers who are present today. I thank every one of you who brought your mothers. Today, I wanted to take up a subject called "The Immeasurable, Limitless Value and Beauty of a Woman."

**The immeasurable limitless value and beauty of a woman.**

The Holy Qur'an, the book of scripture of the Muslims, gives the foundational chapter the number 4, which represents foundation. The 4th surah or chapter of the Qur'an is called *al-Nisa*, "The Women." Later in the 19th surah or chapter, it refers to a very special woman—Maryam, the mother of Jesus, the Messiah.

This Qur'an was not arranged haphazardly. It was divinely arranged so each chapter has significance. The number 4, 440 and 40 are foundational numbers. You can't become president of the United states until you've reached the age of 40. Moses was 40 when he got his command. He was in the wilderness 40 days. All of these are foundational numbers. Something was being done to lay a foundation. Why women? What is a woman the foundation of?

This world in which we live has been destroyed because the woman has been spoiled and laid waste. The Honorable Elijah Muhammad taught us that where there are no decent women, there are no decent men because the woman is the mother of civilization. Civilization is not judged by the man; civilization is judged by the female. The Islamic world needs reform.

You say, "Farrakhan, you speak with authority." It's true because I have authority to speak as I speak. Look at our world of Islam. As elder Muslims, we're losing our children to the world. Why? If the woman can't pray in the mosque with the man—and I'm not saying something that I don't know. I've traveled all over our world, and I have been in parts of our world of Islam where the men were in air-conditioned rooms saying their prayers and the women were out on the dirt making prostration in the hot day's sun in Africa. But in Mecca, women and men are at the Kaaba. In Mecca, they pray [in the same place]. Shouldn't that be the example? What has happened to us, that we have allowed old traditions, cultural traditions to sideswipe the culture of Islam?

The Christian world needs to be reformed in its expression of women. Even the Jewish world needs reform. Some of my, I think well-meaning, Brothers—I'm not sure that what I'm about to say is the absolute truth—but they say that the Taliban, which means "students,"—don't desire that the woman be educated. I don't know that that is the truth but if it is, it is sentencing a nation to death. An ignorant woman is the death of a nation any time a man is afraid to educate a woman, when Allah (God), The Supreme introduces Himself to us as the Best Knower; and deprives one of His creatures of the gift of knowledge, the gift of Qur'anic knowledge. "You stay at home. I'll go and make the prayers and I'll come back and pray for you and the family. Don't worry, I'll study, and I will teach you." That would be good if you were a good student. How dare us arrogate to ourselves that we are fit to teach this Qur'an to the woman that Allah (God)—not you or I—created for you.

## Defending women against desecration

Sisters, you have been devalued in this society. It's heartbreaking to drive down certain streets in major cities and see beautiful women of every color and every race half-nude, selling themselves to anyone who would purchase pleasure from them. They have fallen so low. It doesn't seem that we care. Some men will put their women up to this kind of behavior for the sake of money. I was traveling in Mexico in 1960. I went from Los Angeles to Tijuana. As I was walking the streets of Tijuana, a man said to me, "My daughter, she's 14. Would you like to have sex with my daughter?" As Allah (God) as my witness, it took everything within me to keep me from killing him. I would have ripped his throat out just for offering me his daughter. You may think that is funny.

I was traveling in Africa and one of my African Brothers, who is fairly highly placed, wanted to get a green card. He wanted to know if I, as the representative of the Honorable Elijah Muhammad in America, would allow one of my Sisters to be used so he could get a green card. He's a big man. My son was there. I threatened to kill him in the airport. You say, "Damn, Farrakhan." You're damned right, Farrakhan. Once you are taught of God the value of a woman, then you will kill to keep her safe. It's because you don't know her value or yours that you play with her, devalue her, and laugh at her as she opens her knees to you. You impregnate her and walk away without even a thought of responsibility. Elijah Muhammad put that in me.

I was a young Muslim working in a store in Elmhurst, New York, across the street from a high school. Two white policemen were beating a Black girl. I was keeping the store open; it was in the morning. But when I saw the police beating her, I left the store and challenged them. They thought I was crazy and evidently to them, I was crazy enough to try to protect a female. I warned them—without any F.O.I. [Fruit of Islam] around me—Allah (God) was sufficient for me. I warned them not to put a hand on her. They put her in the car, and I said I'm coming down to the station to make sure. What gives a man that kind of strength that he doesn't fear death? Number one, it's love for your people; and number two, it's knowledge of the value of what that policeman was desecrating.

Who are you, Black woman? We have Muslim Brothers with stores who don't have any respect for you. They say that they are Muslims, but they will sell *khanzir* [pig], they will sell liquor, and they will hit on our women and girls. What kind of Muslim are you that you would take advantage of the ignorant to whom the Prophet sent you to teach? If you are a Muslim, you have a responsibility to those who have never heard, and that is to share with them the beauty of what has transformed your life, not to take advantage of their weakness or wickedness.

## Divine essence

Who are you? Do you really, really know how valued you are in the sight of your Creator? There's a very beautiful scripture in the Holy Qur'an [Surah 4:1]: "O people, keep your duty to your Lord, Who created you from a single being and created its mate of the same kind, and spread from these two many men and women."

Some scholars look at the Arabic word *nafs*, which means "soul" or "essence." If Allah (God) created us from a single essence, what is that essence? How could Allah (God) create man as His khalifah, and the essence of that man is not the essence of Him Who created man? You can't stand in the place of God if that which is in God is not in you. You can't, Biblically speaking, say man and woman are created in the image and likeness of God and the essence of God is not in you.

113

Why did I say the limitless immeasurable value and beauty of a woman? Some women may look in the mirror and say, "I'm not so pretty." Some women are not physically attractive, but physical attractiveness is not beauty. That's why I said the "limitless immeasurable value and beauty" not of *some* women, of women.

God created us from a single essence, but He didn't say what the essence was. He left that for those who would study to determine what that essence was. Most Muslims, in error, think that there is no divine essence in the human being. That's erroneous thinking. That's why you're so quick to kill each other. You don't see your evil to one another is your evil to God Himself.

This is borne out in the scriptures of the Bible and Qur'an. The Qur'an says [Surah 5:32] that when you kill a human being, it's like killing all men; and when you save a human being, it is like saving all men. What is so great about that one man, that by killing him, you kill all? Look at what trouble we're in today. We kill for the joy of killing. Life in the inner cities is devalued because one brother will kill another. One sister will kill another. One man will kill his wife. One wife will kill her husband. We don't stop to think of God's view.

The beauty of the woman is the matchless beauty of God. This is you, on the inside. The Honorable Elijah Muhammad taught us where the Qur'an says that Allah is not begotten, nor does He beget, He's self-created. He doesn't have a mother. If He had a mother, He was begotten. If He doesn't have a mother, then how did He get here?

He, in His limitless wisdom and power, created Himself in triple darkness, so teaches the Honorable Elijah Muhammad. He said we don't know how long it took Him because nothing was there to measure time. He created Himself, then studied Himself; and out of Himself, He made a second Self. The Bible says the woman comes from the man. The Qur'an says the same. Sister, you are from us, but more importantly, not us: you are from Allah (God).

114

## Unlocking nature

I have studied birth and creation. There's always pain involved in the creative process. I don't know how He did it, but I know it had to be painful. "Farrakhan, just a minute. How do you know these things?" I know because He made each one of us a witness of Himself.

Yesterday, a child showed me pictures of the baby being formed in her womb. She said, "Look, grandpa, see?" I didn't know what I was looking at, but I looked at her and how joyous she was over something she didn't have anything to do with. **She did not have anything to do with what Allah (God) was creating in her womb.** It's like a self-creation after the order of God.

The intelligence in the sperm seeks the egg. How could it be looking for something that it didn't know what it was looking at. There is intelligence in the sperm. Whose intelligence? Whose intelligence is in the sperm when it seeks to form the first cell of life? it's not your intelligence. You didn't know what was going on. It's not my intelligence. It's God's essence, His intelligence. The Quran says I—not you, not I—I [God] created you in the womb. He doesn't give that honor to anyone but Himself. "I created you in the womb and little it is that you give thanks." He says: "I created you from cloudy water." "I created you from dust, then a clot."

Which one of you mothers said, "Now it's time for this to be a clot?" You had nothing to do with it. Hands were forming, head was forming. Eyes and ears and fingers and toes and heart were forming, and we had nothing to do with it, Brother. This is God working in the womb. That's how sacred your womb is. No man should have access to the sacredness of your womb unless that man is worthy, not because he's cute, not because he is popular, not because he has a little money. Your womb is too precious to throw it away. That is worse than casting pearls before swine.

The Qur'an is like a key to unlock nature so we can master nature. That's why al-Fatihah opens the Qur'an and it's called al miftah, "the key." It opens nature for us. Allah (God) says in the Qur'an, He created the woman that the man may find peace and quiet of mind in her. He created her as solace. We used to call these big things that we would play our records in "the console." That's a heck of a thing that we would find consolation in the console—and consolation in her.

Why did He make that nature in you? Coming out of pain, toil, and hard labor, there is a need for comfort. A woman is to be a comfort to a man who is a man. (Sisters clap loudly) I messed up on that one. Brothers, when I speak like this, look over at her and see how she's reacting because she's known this is the truth.

## The proper exercise of control

The Qur'an tells you [Surah 2:223] that the woman is your tilth, she's your treasure. So, you may go into her as you like but "send good beforehand for yourselves"—we forgot that part. It's a heck of a thing when a man acts ugly, mistreating the woman all through the day, being nasty, but when the sun goes down, he wants some pleasure.

There was a judge in Saudi Arabia that said it was alright for a man to rape his wife. What kind of a man is that? Who the h-- wants a woman who doesn't want us. You have made yourself a dog. "What the h---. Let's get it on" and she'll say, "Well, hurry up and get it over with because I'm tired. I have to go to work in the morning while you're sitting around watching TV." If this resembles any person living or dead, it's not a coincidence.

Brothers and Sisters, she is a divine creature. Notice how women gravitate toward men who are stars, potential stars. You almost go out of your mind trying to get the star—the star basketball player, the star singer, the star corporate executive. Whoever it is, you want a star because you're the woman of God. You strive for the best. Even if you can't obtain it, you have thoughts in your mind as to how you would like to console or comfort somebody that you feel is worthy.

Sisters, this is why Satan is always after the woman. He can't bring the man down unless he goes through the woman. If Satan's desire is to create an adverse world, he must beguile and deceive the woman. It is not wrong in the Islamic world that we keep our women away from strange men. That's good wisdom.

You don't go to a Muslim Brother's house and ask, "Can I see your wife?" "I thought you came here to see me. What business is it of yours to see my wife?" When I visited the Muslim world, the highest honor that they could pay to a stranger was to let him be in the presence of the women and daughters of that family. We were in the palaces of the kings and great sultans, but you'd never see a woman. They have Brothers who serve. If you want tea or coffee, the Brothers will bring it. That's good. Why? Women can't help themselves; they have wandering eyes like we do. "Who's that in there? Who did daddy bring?" You hear whispering behind the curtain, "He sure is cute."

A woman is so sacred. In his 1957 Saviour's Day address, the Honorable Elijah Muhammad taught on three words: the respect, control, and protection of the so-called Negro woman. Women don't mind respect, but don't talk about control. But you can never protect a woman that you can't control. Sisters, I know you say, "No man is going to control me." You're not going to mind being controlled if the man is under the control of God.

God regulates the affairs of everything that He creates, and He does it by means of law. When He takes woman from man and gives the woman to the man as his second self, He also gives the man the responsibility to maintain her in all aspects of her creation.

When a man is a good maintainer of a woman, she doesn't mind. If she's a good woman, she doesn't mind his exercise of control because a man under the control of God is not going to be wicked in the way he exercises his authority. He'll be just, he will be fair, and he will listen to his wife. If truth is spoken from his wife, he must bow to truth not to her biology, but to the fact that she's telling the truth. Truth is uppermost in the mind of a true servant of God.

## Cultivating the beauty within

When Satan gets a hold of the woman, he encourages, exacerbates, and makes mischief with her natural power to give consolation and solace to a man. The woman of God is so different from the woman that has been captured by Satan. The woman of God knows her beauty, her form. The breasts and backside of a woman are embellishments of her body—very attractive to the eye of a man even if he wants to be right. it is hard as heck to be right when a woman is displaying her finery in your presence.

The Qur'an holds all the prophets sinless, but the Bible said Solomon saw this woman. He wasn't trying to look for her; he just looked out and there she was. You can imagine—he's a prophet of God! According to the Bible, he sent that woman's husband into battle to be killed so he could get the man's wife.

Some may say, "Well, you know, the Qur'an doesn't talk like that." It's a beautiful book, this Qur'an. I'm going to tell you what I see. No man is sinless, but God holds His prophets sinless because He guards and guides them. If God were to put in the Qur'an the mistakes of the prophets, how would that be a guide to you and me to be better? It doesn't mean that prophets don't make mistakes. Allah (God) covers their mistakes.

Here is the beauty of what I am saying. It was a full moon last night. The prophets, represented in symbolic language, is the moon because the moon has no light of its own. It reflects the light of the sun in the absence of the sun. But the moon has a dark side. God never allows the dark side of the moon to face the earth because it's the light reflected from the moon that equalizes the waters of the earth and ripens the crops. If you turned it where only the dark side of the room was shown, then the waters would not be balanced, and the crops would not be ripened. So, God keeps the face of light to the earth, and He keeps the best of the prophets to the people so that they are examples of the best of what human beings can achieve.

The prophet I referenced was David, not Solomon; Solomon was the result. Thank you, thank you. We're not allowed to make mistakes in front of the people. If you make a mistake and it's unintentional, you know the truth of it, then somebody must point it out so you will never misinform the people. Thank you so much.

When Satan gets the woman, she knows her power. I've watched young girls as they come into puberty. You see their breasts developing, you see their form developing. I don't know whether it's intentional, but I watch when they come in the presence of men [demonstrates sticking out their chest]. That's why we don't let our girls in the presence of men. When they begin to discover their powers of attraction, they want to see how attractive they are. Satan is getting into the house. Satan is creeping up into a woman who is beginning to know her power of attraction but not her value.

The Bible says [Proverbs 31:10] a virtuous woman is more precious than silver or gold. How many virtuous women are in the world that we live in today? It's a thing of the past. Girls are having sex at eight, nine, 10, and 11 years of age. The Honorable Elijah Muhammad said, "There's no such thing as a no-good woman. Every no-good woman was made no good by a no-good man." A young girl, seeing her body forming, wants to know, "Do you see me? Am I desirable?" The man, if he's a good man, looks away because he realizes that this beautiful child does not know her value. Her value is not in her bosom. Her value is not in her buttocks. Her value is not in the prettiness of her face. Her value is in the beauty of God that's hidden within her that has to be cultivated.

## The real House of God

God, through the Messiah and the Mahdi, wants to make a new people out of us. I want you to pay close attention to this. The Kaaba, the qibla or the spiritual center of Muslims, features a stone that is called the Black Stone. It's a simple cube of cinder block. It is in the eastern corner of the Kaaba. All Muslims who are blessed to go to Mecca want to kiss the Black Stone. Prophet Muhammad kissed it. I think it was Ali who said, "I kiss it not because it has power, but I kiss it because the Prophet himself kissed it." The

Kaaba is a sign of a house. It is an ancient house that's a sign of something bigger than itself.

You are a stone. I am a stone. We are stones, mortared together in the love of Allah (God), His messenger, Islam. That makes us into an impenetrable building that becomes the real House of God. Mecca is not more beautiful than you. Most Muslims are taken out by the beauty of Mecca. It's true, it's beautiful. So is Rome, beautiful. But which building made by the hands of man equals in beauty the building fashioned by Allah (God)? There's none. You are the real House of God. In the end times, the Mahdi is going to fashion the Kingdom of Islam from a stone in the corner that is a Black stone, but not quite black; it is yellowish brown. That stone is like the cornerstone. The Bible [1 Peter 2:6] calls it a precious cornerstone laid in Zion. The Mahdi or the Messiah can't make a new people, a holy people without making a new and holy woman. You are the candidates for that.

## Making great men

Satan has us now but look at how the righteous women of the East dressed where we came from or were brought from. Did they wear miniskirts? They didn't? Did they wear bras with halter tops with their middle out and hip-huggers, calling themselves the righteous? How could a preacher preach when you come into the church and sit down with your dress to your hip. He doesn't have to say like the Masons, "I spied Mecca," because whatever he was spying, your dress knocked out his subject.

Sisters, you are candidates to be the women again of God. When you know who you are, you inspect men thoroughly. If I ask you, why do you like this man? "I was hot and bothered one night." What is it that you see in him? Does he have a job? He doesn't work but you're interested. You have a job. You have a car. He's driving your car and living in your apartment. What can he do for you? After a while, don't you get tired of trying to give solace and comfort to a bum? I'm not putting us down, Brothers. A man is not worth anything if he will live off a woman. That's just not the way God intended things to be.

Proverbs 10:1 says, "A wise son maketh a glad father, but a foolish son is the heaviness of his mother." These are the proverbs of Solomon. I want you to think about it: a wise son makes a glad father, but a foolish son is the heaviness of his mother. This is how valuable a woman is in making great men. I didn't have a father. I had a great mother. My mother was a strong woman. My brother and I didn't get any checks from our fathers. My father never bought me as much as a shoelace, but I thank Allah (God) for him because without him I wouldn't be. But he did nothing for me.

My mother, she did it all. She was not a foolish mother. I never saw my mother engaged in foolishness. I never got up before my mother. When she put me to bed, she was still working. She didn't care if the men in her life did not support her children. She said she would do it herself. We were on welfare. When I graduated from high school at 16 years of age, I came home and my mother said, "I got this check from welfare. I want you to come with me." She went to the welfare office and gave the check back to the welfare person, and told them, "I thank you for helping me to get my son this far. I'll take it from here." That's a wise woman.

She was a strong woman. She beat me; there was no playing in that house. She wore this backside out, but she always beat me for a principle. One of the things that she would beat me for more than anything that I did was when I lied about what I did. I couldn't fool her. She would trap me in my lie, beat me for what I did, and then beat the h-- out of me for the lie. What was she doing? She was beating into me a love for truth. She was making me into a man who would not be afraid of the consequences of telling the truth.

God cannot use you if you fear men as we ought to fear Allah (God). If we were unafraid, we could raise a nation better than what we are doing.

A serpent was after the woman in Genesis, but a dragon was after the woman in the Book of Revelation. In the Book of

Revelation [12:5], the woman was pregnant with a man-child that was going to rule the nations with a rod of iron. Sisters, sometimes you are too weak to make a man-child for God because you compromise too much with that that devalues you.

You are full of foolishness, sitting in front of the television, watching silly programs and reality shows. What do you get out of it except that which makes you more and more foolish. You look at Beyoncé, but you don't see the value in Beyonce as a woman of God. When you look at Beyoncé, you know what you're looking at. Sisters, if that's what you like—to shake your backside and learn how to shake it better than the other sister that's shaking, so you can get on the dance floor and show men how valuable the booty is—how depraved is your real beauty.

A wise son maketh a glad father. Sisters, you're going to have to be stronger than you are. You are much too weak. **You are much too weak** compromising with a world that God is taking out. Do you know how you got to be this way? When the White man made our fathers slaves, his aim was to destroy us as a people. He never let our parents teach us our language, our culture, our history, our religion, our true nationality, our God. He stripped us of all of that by taking our original parents away from us, then he raised us.

Hitler wanted to make a new Aryan race—blond hair, blue eyes, superior White people. He had an idea, but he had to search among the women to see if his idea was taking root in them. Sometimes he would take German children from their mothers and rear them under teachers that were wedded to his ideology.

What about God? Do you think that God would be pleased with us, bringing these children into the world?

## The womb of the mind

If you look at your children, they're very special these days. Have you noticed how smart they are? Have you noticed their level of intelligence? Have you noticed the curiosity in these children? But if they have a weak or foolish mother, she will involve these children in foolish pursuit. We want to be like the woman that the dragon was after, who had in her womb a man-child that was going to rule the nations with a rod of iron.

May Allah (God) bless the womb of every one of you, my dear Sisters, who are expecting. Don't engage in a lot of foolishness as you are making new life. You're marking your baby with foolishness. Be serious about the life that is growing within you. You can make it into a likeness of God. The Bible says [Psalm 82:6]: "Ye are all god, children of The Most High God." It's going to take a strong mother to make a child like that.

Don't doubt yourself. You have the ability. You must start now putting off foolishness and filling your head with knowledge. The more knowledge you have, the more you can see something great for what is growing within you and project it onto the one that's growing within you, the child will come from your womb born to achieve. That's why we named this mosque, "Maryam," because Jesus, the Messiah is probably one of the greatest human beings who ever lived.

I call it "Mosque Maryam" because everyone that comes here, I'm going to impregnate you with an idea that's bigger than the foolishness. When it gestates and grows in your mind, when you go out into that crazy world, you will go out as a saviour, as a deliverer. From this day forward, make no merchandise of your women and girls. Treat them with respect and honor even if they don't deserve it because, underneath all their foolishness, they are God's child.

May Allah (God) bless each and every one of you. Thank you for coming. Thank you for listening as I greet you in peace, *As-Salaam Alaikum.*

# 7 THE DIVINE VALUE OF WOMEN

In The Name of Allah, The Beneficent, The Merciful. We give Him praise and thanks for His Mercy and His Goodness to the members of the human family that whenever any member of this family strays from His straight path and earns His displeasure or His wrath, before He punishes, He always raises from among that people a prophet or a messenger to whom He gives what is called "divine revelation" in the form of scripture. Through the scriptures, He guides people back to His straight path that they might once again come into His Divine Favor.

We thank Allah (God) for Moses and the Israelite prophets who gave us the Old Testament. We thank Him for Jesus and the apostles who gave us the Gospel and the New Testament. We thank Him for Muhammad ibn Abdullah, the son of Abdullah, through whom Allah (God) revealed the last book to come to the human family, which is called the Holy Qur'an.

I am a student of the Honorable Elijah Muhammad, and I could never thank Allah (God) enough for His intervention in our affairs in the Person of Master Fard Muhammad Who came among us, as it was written that God would search and find that sheep that was lost. He would bring that sheep again to Himself, that the bottom rail would come to the top, and the last would become the first, and the tail would become the head. The scripture says, "This is the Lord's doing and it is marvelous in our sight." We never believed that we were worthy enough in our condition that God would bring us from the bottom to the top, that God would take the tail and make it the head, that God would favor us, not by sending someone but by coming Himself.

As it is written that God visited Egypt, He didn't send Moses, He came and raised Moses and then missioned him to Pharoah to free His people. You are in a worse condition than the Children of Israel because you have been under a wicked oppressor not just for a day or week or year or month, but for over four centuries living under the shadow of death without justice.

I thank Him for His Coming and for His wise choice of one from among us, the Honorable Elijah Muhammad. I'm honored and happy beyond words today to greet each and every one of you with the greeting words of peace. We say it in the Arabic language and in the words that Jesus and the prophets always spoke to their disciples. Jesus didn't say, "Hi, how ya' doing? What's happening, dog?" Jesus was a man of peace. In him is the essence of peace. He comes to end this turbulent world of bloodshed and strife and hatred to bring in an eternal Kingdom where everyone who would be in that Kingdom would enjoy the greatest gift of all—peace and contentment of mind.

I thank Him for the Honorable Elijah Muhammad. I greet all of you with the greeting words of peace in the original language of the scriptures Hebrew and Arabic, *As-Salam Alaikum* in Arabic, *Shalom Aleichem* in Hebrew. But of course, we don't speak Arabic or Hebrew, so we just say peace be unto you.

I want to thank you all for coming. There are hardly any men in here at all. This is your day. I have a lot to say to men and they're filling up the gymnasium. The gymnasium is full of men. Don't feel bad, men, that you are not here today. God cannot make us the head if the woman is not lifted. If God does not lift a woman, the man will never come up. If God is going to make a new world and a better world, He's going to make that world coming through a woman. Remember that.

125

I want to thank all of those who worked so hard on the Vanguard program—thank you. Thank you to the mothers who allowed their young daughters to come. I thank you all for your visit to the farm yesterday. What you don't know when you left, some of the females of my family—children, grandchildren—were talking about the message that we gave yesterday: the tone of the message, the sternness of the message, the correctness of the message and the effect that the message had on their hearts. Someone ran into the house and said, "Come! Come quickly!"

As my family ran out, I was the last to come out. They said that the wheels, the UFOs, were out on the farm. When I went out, they were there—not one, not two, not three, not four, not five, not eight—and they put on a show for us. Many members of my family broke into tears of joy because they've heard about these things. I have taught them about these things but many of them had not seen them. But they made themselves very, very visible and it was like an exclamation point to my talk to you. It was as though God was smiling on you for accepting the role of a woman and accepting righteousness as your way of life.

## Our essence determines our character

There will never be a righteous Kingdom until and unless there is a righteous woman. Where there are no decent women, there are no decent men, for the woman, the Honorable Elijah Muhammad teaches—the Black woman in particular—is the Mother of Civilization. Today I wanted to talk about the divine nature and value of women. No matter your color or race or ethnicity, you have never looked at yourself as a part of The Divine. That will change today.

We live in the creation of God. Whatever God creates is of Himself. If God is the Author and Source of divinity, how could He create a universe and that universe not be divine. You can't improve on anything that He created. He created it perfect. He didn't create the sun in His image neither the moon nor the stars. He created nothing in His image or likeness but the human being. How could you be in His image and after His likeness and not have His divine nature? Some of my Brothers and Sisters, Islamic scholars, they don't want to think that the human has divine qualities. We can wrangle over that with any scholar in the world. Why are you justified in wearing the Attributes of God if you cannot reflect those attributes that are divine? We want to acquaint you today with your divinity and then call on you to be yourself.

In the Qur'an, the fourth surah or chapter says something that I would like us to consider. The chapter is called, "The Women." The women. You haven't read any chapter in the Bible called the women. Though you have read about great women in the Bible, not a whole chapter is dedicated to women. That's not the only one. There's a whole chapter in the Qur'an dedicated to Mary, the mother of Jesus. In that chapter, the angels were in dispute among themselves as to who would have charge of Mary. according to the Qur'an. Mary was the best of women—not the mother of Abraham, not the mother of Moses, not the mother of Muhammad, but the mother of Jesus.

Let me help you to know why Mary is an example for women. She was not an unchaste woman even though the Jews charged her with fornication and even referred to her offspring as an illegitimate child. She had to be secretly put away because the Jews at that time, immersed in the Law of Moses, if they saw the woman pregnant but did not see a man, they would have charged her and killed her. So, God protected her. The Qur'an says (Surah 21:91; Surah 23:50) Jesus and his mother were a sign. A sign points to something bigger than itself.

In this chapter of the Qur'an (Surah 4:1) it reads, "In The Name of Allah, The Beneficent, The Merciful. O people, keep your duty to your Lord, Who created you from a single being and created its mate of the same kind, and spread from these two many men and women." Some translations of the Arabic don't say "being" but uses "essence." Surely God created you from a single essence and created your mate of the same. What is the essence of something?

According to the dictionary, the essence of a thing is the intrinsic nature or indispensable quality of that thing, especially something abstract that determines its character. Here's God creating a human, the first human, from a single essence and created the woman of the same. If God created us from the same essence, then what is that essence that determines our character? The essence of you is God Himself.

The essence—that which determines your character—is your connection to the Creator of the heavens and the earth, Who is also your and my Creator. You have never looked at yourself as belonging to God. You only see yourself in the light of what the enemy has made you to see yourself—as ex-slaves or Black people of no worth or value or purpose in life. He never taught you.

I don't blame him because he was given power to rule. His time is up. Your time has come. God has come to bring you back to yourself, to introduce you to your intrinsic nature, essence—the essence that determines your character.

The essence that determines our character is God Himself and the meaning of character is the mental and moral qualities distinctive to an individual. **The mental and moral qualities that are distinctive to the human being.** That's very, very heavy. If your moral character and mental character are of God, then you must ask yourself what happened to us that our morals are not where God wants them to be. Our mental qualities have been curtailed, brought down or even killed. What happened to women and men, that we are so far down and away from the essence of our own being, that we now are not even a caricature of what God intended?

Look at the Book of Genesis when you go home. I know you love the Bible, but you don't read it enough. It's not a book that should be in your house like something that you put up to keep devils away. It's a book to be read. It's a book to be studied. It's a book to be acted upon. The Book of Genesis tells us about the beginnings of things. That's what "genesis" means: beginning. It starts with the creation of the world and every living creature in it. It records the first marriage, the first sin, the first consequences of sin, and the first reference to God's future plan to redeem humanity. After it recounts the stories of the flood and the Tower of Babel, Genesis also tells the story of the birth of a nation. We are now in our genesis.

## The nature of our creation

I'd like to read a few things from the Bible that helps you see your divine nature, our divine nature. The Bible says (Genesis 1:1-5), "God created the heavens and the earth, the earth was without form, and void; and darkness was upon the face of the deep. And the Spirit of God moved upon the face of the waters. And God said, Let there be light: and there was light… And God separated the light from the darkness. And God called the light Day, and the darkness He called Night." He created the sun the greater light and the moon the lesser light (Genesis 1:16). It talks about creating the firmament (Genesis 1:6-8). He starts with the heavens. That's very important because if you don't create the heavens, the earth has no existence. The earth exists because of its relationship to the heavens.

And God said let the waters beneath the sky flow together into one place so dry ground may appear. And God called the dry ground Land, and the waters He called seas. And God saw that it was good. Then He said let the lands sprout with vegetation, every sort of seed-bearing plant. (Genesis 1:9-12)

God was really preparing a heaven for the righteous. When you were born, you were born into this, like Adam. All of this was in existence before Adam was even made. When Adam was made, God had prepared everything for him. He did all of this great work in five days. On the 6th day, He said let me make a man. Most of the time, we think that when He made a man, it was just the male figure. Not true. Let me show you what the scripture says.

The 26th verse (Genesis) reads: "God said, Let us make man in our image, after our likeness: and let them have dominion" over the fowl, the fish, the birds, the livestock, all wild animals. It says (Genesis 1:27) God created human beings in His own image, "in the

image of God created He him; male and female, created He them."
When you're looking at Adam as the offspring of God, look again at
yourself because it wasn't just man that was created; it was man and
woman. The fifth chapter of Genesis says (verse 2), "male and female
created He them; ... and called their name Adam." So when we talk
about man, you can't even talk about a man unless a woman is
present because there would be no man without a woman. Let's deal
with this.

When God created this man and this woman, He gave them
assignments. He didn't tell you to go to the nightclub, hang out in the
bar, get drunk and fornicate. He gave you instructions that come out
of the very nature of your creation. Be fruitful. What do you think
that means? Everything else that He created, He created it to
reproduce after its own kind. If He created the cattle and they
reproduce cattle, the birds reproduce birds, the fowl reproduce fowl,
the beasts of the field reproduce beasts of the field, then man and
woman do what? Reproduce themselves. But if you are in the image
and likeness of God, then He too is being reproduced every time you
properly reproduce. Think now, think with me.

He tells you, male and female, "I'm giving you dominion."
You can't be stupid and rude. He never intended for a woman to be
ignorant. He never intended for a woman to be unlearned or
uneducated. If you are unlearned and uneducated, you cannot fulfill
your destiny.

## The degradation of women

The enemy wanted you dumb. The enemy wants you to think
nothing of yourself so the enemy strips you of your real nature. He
has de-natured the female and the male. Any time somebody
denatures you, they devalue you. Right now, as a woman or as a
Black man, you are not valued. The worst part of that is you don't
value yourself.

He's made us think so little of who we are, the word b**** is
a common expression among us. "Oh my God, Farrakhan, you

cursed." No, I wasn't cussing. That b****. What are you saying? What are you calling yourself? Should any woman be referred to as a b**** when a b**** is a female dog? If you will use that kind of language to your sister or some other woman, you have devalued her. In devaluing her, you have devalued yourself and you have devalued your mother.

Jimmy Hoffa's son, James Hoffa Jr. was talking the other day. You might have heard this on *CNN* or *Fox News*. He was talking about the unions and said, "Let's get rid of those sons of b******." That sounds awful coming from such a high place, but what is he saying. If you are the son of a b****, you are a dog. God said He made these creatures, but did He make you a dog? or who made you a dog?

There is a song *Who Let The Dogs Out*. Who let the dogs out? When they drop a woman down to the position of a sex object and then take your clothes off so that men will see the beauty of your form and become sexually stimulated and aroused by the way you dress, you have made yourself a dog and you're bringing the dog out of men. I know that's not what you want to do but that's the vogue now. "I'm sexy. I want to be sexy." Everything that the enemy puts before you is to make you sexually attractive to a man. You're in so much pain because you attracted a dog. You attracted a man that acts like a dog and he made a b**** out of you.

Elijah Muhammad said to us that the nature of the woman is to equal herself up to God. She will strive always to be better. But if she got a no-good man, the Honorable Elijah Muhammad said there's no such thing as a no-good woman. Every no-good woman was made no-good by a no-good man.

My dear Sisters, we are the children of slaves. The slave master had a purpose for us that was not the aim of God. He had freedom when we were on the plantation to go in and out of us sexually. Whether we wanted to give ourselves or not, he took it from us. When you look at yourself on the screen today in Hollywood and other places, how does Hollywood portray not only our women but white women as well? They keep you looking—they call it in the Jewish language of what I've read of what they want to make of you in the movies—a tart. A tart is something sweet and nice, delicious, delectable, delightful. After dinner, a tart.

They want to make of you—a woman who was created in the image of God—they want to make you such that you will come down, way down, bring your man down, teach your children in a way that they will be down, and you will look at yourself in your nakedness and enjoy seeing yourself in a degraded state.

When I talked about my beautiful little Sister Rihanna or Beyonce or the other beautiful young lady that I can't call her name, She's a fine-looking child. That child is well-appointed. Lord, did I say something wrong? When you think that your bosom and your backside are your stock in trade that makes you valuable, then you will strip down and show miss booty. I've read when President Obama got elected, a Black woman in the papers in Chicago talked about how the First Lady of the nation "got back." What in the world are we thinking about that we measure the value of a woman by the shape of her backside? Is this who you are? Is this what you want to be? Or do you want something better than what the White man has made of you?

The divine nature and value of a woman. What is it when these men want to propose, you see them on TV and the man gets down on his knees, gets out a little ring from Kay Jewelers or Walmart, and proposes. Do you know what that means? It means that, in that act, he recognizes your supreme value. He gets down on his knees. Oh, my God, if you could just read what that really means. You are so valuable that a man should never have you just to have you. He must be worthy of you or he's not worth having you. That's the last time that man got down on his knees with honor and respect. He wants you to come to him. He wants you to give yourself to him, so he will act in a way to make you give yourself.

There's hardly a man out here who is worthy of you giving away yourself to him. There's some out there who are worthy but, if you are not looking for worthy, you get what you get. You do not look for someone worthy of you because you have no self-worth. So, any man who looks good, any man who talks good, can get you to lie down with him.

Let me say something that I said to the Vanguard yesterday. Almighty God created everything out of the dark womb of space. He gives you a womb that resembles the darkness of space out of which everything is created. Man doesn't have a womb. It's you. Your womb is the workshop of God. Every king, every ruler, every prophet, every wise man or woman, every scientist, every general, every person of value came through the womb of a woman.

The most precious womb was the womb of Mary. Her womb was the workshop of God. From her womb, God produced that one who would reconcile the whole of humanity back to Himself. For you who loved Jesus, Jesus was not loved by this world. You can't love Jesus and not live the life that Jesus asked you to live. *(responding to applause):* I'm very full.

## A guarded channel

Your womb is a special place. The vaginal tract of the female is the entry to the womb. That is sacred. That tract is protected by a thin piece of flesh. It's not easily accessible. There's pain and there's blood when you enter that sacred chamber. I know you have never heard a preacher preach like this.

As my Father Elijah Muhammad said, they couldn't preach it because they didn't know it. But today, you will know that I have a teacher who loves you so much that he will absolutely train us, and is training us, to protect you with our lives.

I'm going back now to the sacred passageway. Geopolitics may be a little heavy in a sense but look at the Panama Canal. It took billions of dollars to create from the Isthmus of Panama, a canal that would link the Atlantic Ocean to the Pacific Ocean so that travelers would not have to go all the way around the tip of South America to come into the Pacific Ocean. That channel is so valuable that armies protect it. [President Jimmy] Carter gave it back to the Panamanians. When [President Ronald] Reagan became president, he said, "We're going to get the Panama Canal back." Under General Colin Powell, they attacked Panama, killed more than 4,000 Black and Brown people in order to destroy Panama's ability to protect that channel.

The Suez Canal unites the Mediterranean Sea to the Red Sea, down into the Gulf of Aden. On the other side is another strategic waterway that links Pakistan, Iran, and the Emirates with the Persian Gulf into the Indian Ocean. Geopolitically, these canals are so valuable that they fight for the advantage to be in both places so they can govern, monitor, control and even keep ships that they don't like from using those waterways. That's how valuable channels are.

The channel to the womb is a sacred channel that must be guarded. The Qur'an says guard your chastity. Guard it. When you leave that channel unguarded, you may open yourself up to diseased men, people who don't care or have any value for you but just use you as a pleasure tool and then throw you away. Some of you do not think that you will get a man unless you lay down and open your knees to that man. If you have to open your knees to get a man, that isn't a man. He's not worthy of you.

Let me tell you something about men—which you already know; you could tell me. When you are easy for a man to get, he is not the man who wants to marry and spend his life with you. He's the man you'll come to when he wants pleasure but he's not the man who will give you the type of love, honor, and respect for which you yearn. You'll never get it if that channel is like a free channel. You must pay a lot of money to use the Panama Canal. Nothing is free. Free love doesn't make sense, but you do it in other ways. You know how you do. After a man has access to the channel, after a while you tell him about your rent, phone bill and car note. Pleasure isn't free.

These channels cost money. Before they allow a ship in that channel, they stop you. When we were going through the Panama Canal, I didn't realize how much money the ship had to pay to use it. They stopped you right there. You must come up with what you got to come up with or they won't allow you to go through. That's the way you must be when a man talks about how he loves you. Love is a verb. It isn't a noun. There must be some action behind "I love you."

When you're going through the channel, you must bring your papers. They examine your papers and ask, "Is this ship legally registered? Under what flag are you flying? What is the cargo that you're carrying?" After you satisfy all the requirements and you are verified that you can use that channel, the last thing is the money. Everything else is fine but now, "the price is…"

Your value should never be determined by dollars, but you don't need a man who doesn't have money. You don't need a man if you must work to maintain him. You don't need any man like that.

## Responsibility, courtship, and sex

To the Brothers—Brothers, don't get angry with your Brother. Because you're not worth a d*** if you make babies and you will not support them. I want the register of the Nation to be cleaned up. If you are not feeding your children, you can't occupy any place here. You make babies and you don't care for them. You can party and buy fine shoes and designer clothes, but your children are raggedy, hungry, and out of doors. What kind of man is that? No man will hold a position in the Nation who has babies that he's not taking care of.

I want all Laborers examined. You can stay. We're not putting you out. But what kind of example are we setting if we can occupy positions and talk all this talk and some woman out there is crying because we have failed in our responsibility. We don't need a White man judge to tell us you have to give something. It should come from your heart.

When God gave man and woman dominion, He gave us the power to influence the course of events. He gave us the ability internally, intrinsically, and naturally to manage affairs. He gave us a means of limiting or regulating something. He gave us a place where things are verified.

I like that word "verification." When something is verified that means it's true. You must verify these men. You must manage yourself. You must control yourself. You must be strong enough to regulate the affairs of yourself for when a suitor comes. We call it "courtship" in Islam. I don't know what you call it.

"Court" means you must present evidence so that we will know should I or should I not. You've got to ask the right questions. "I really like you, Sister. You're so beautiful?" *Have you been married before?* "Well, uh uh, yes." *And how many children do you have?* "Well, from Sadie, I have two. From Mindy, I have one." *Two different mothers?* "Well, well, yeah." *And what happened?*

If you had a car wreck, you would want to know what happened to cause the car to wreck because it may not be worth buying. Don't you want a car that has never been in an accident before? Look at all these accidents. We are in a mosque or church with accidents. We see a woman walking up for communion, looking fine. There's no regulation on her dress so when she goes to take communion, she's showing her body. When a female demonstrates her desire for a man in that way, what you see is exactly what you get. Every man likes beauty and you like beauty, too. We're both attractive to each other. But without you guarding your chastity, men are never going to be anything.

People think that in Islam we enslave our women by asking them, not making them, to lower the hem of their garment, to cover their bodies. Some women think, "I ain't never gonna be a Moslem if that's what you Moslems do." But how many movies have you seen about Jesus? Every Easter and every Christmas, there's a movie about Jesus. Which one of the women who was around Jesus came with a miniskirt. Which one of them had their cleavage out to attract Jesus? They all dressed covered.

The beauty of a woman and her body is for her to share with that person that is found worthy of her. No one else. So, when you want to show people what you've got, you're making yourself an object. You like to hear a man whistle at you. Men don't whistle at women. They whistle for dogs. They're dog-calling. That's not what you want.

Your mind is akin to the Mind of God. Women can create. Women can govern. Women can manage. Women can do practically everything that a man does. You're not limited. But you can limit yourself by the way you carry yourself. You must verify a man before you ever, ever, ever permit him access to you.

Like when I talked about the ship, you must be like that person at the canal making sure that this boat is worthy to go through. If you are not strong enough as a woman to question a man, then you will get from the court what you deserve. Some of you feel that you will lose your man if you question him too hard. You won't lose a man; you will lose a dog. And you weren't looking for a dog.

Men should take the same approach. Sisters can look real pretty but they've been married three times. Three wrecks. You'd better ask some questions. "What caused the breakup with husband number one? Husband number 2? Husband number 3. Maybe I don't want to be husband number 4." Your breakups have in them the reality of something missing in us on both sides that could not keep our marriage together. So courting is important. Don't let any man get to you until you have satisfied the inquiry, the curious nature.

After you submit yourself to a man and he enters that channel and you become pregnant, then you can't find him anymore, you're locked into two things. "Should I have the baby?" Since the government has accepted that abortion is legal, "should I kill a life because I don't really want responsibility." The act of sex is a responsible act. The act of sex that procreates human life means once you enter that, you must sacrifice for the life with which you're pregnant. You can't be a party mama and drop your irresponsible behavior on your mother. Your mother raised you, now she has to raise your children, too?

**Women are fundamental like the earth**

There are three things that Jews have done that makes them

the most powerful, richest, and influential people on our planet. In the Babylonian Talmud, Jews are told, "you must acquire land." So, no matter where they are in the world, you'll always find Jewish people having land, real estate, and cash that they invest. They are in trade, commerce, and banking, and the whole world has to come to them. The Honorable Elijah Muhammad said to study the White man. He's successful. He makes no excuses for his failure. He works in a collective manner. Elijah Muhammad said you do the same.

We left the South because farming was drudgery. When you had to sharecrop, that was painful. When many of our Brothers and Sisters left Mississippi, Alabama, Georgia, and Arkansas, they didn't want to see a farm anymore. We got stuck in factories, but the factories were run by the relations of the people that we worked for on the plantation. They hooked it up. You ran from the farm to the factory, but the same people who had your grandpa and grandma picking cotton, tobacco, and sugar on the plantation was running the factory. The enemy has you coming and going.

Those who know sharecropping, whenever you came to the end of a season to tell that man, "Here's what I have in my books," he told you, "Wait a minute. You owe me and you better not figure behind me." Many of our people suffered indescribable pain from working on the land. The enemy destroyed in us value for land.

Elijah Muhammad said that the woman is the *field* through which we produce our nation. He describes you as "earth." Earth is fundamental to everything. Everything. And so are you.

I didn't tell the Sisters when they were at the farm yesterday about what we are learning from a man named Mr. Will Allen in Milwaukee about producing soil. We met this great, great Brother. He visited the farm and said that's nice, but no matter how good the seed is, if you don't have good soil, you won't get the best product. I sent a team to learn his methods. Of them was my daughter, my son-in-law and another son, and other believers. They learned how to create soil. They learned how to look at soil and determine its value. When you put your hand in soil and there are no worms, that's not good soil.

One of our farmers from Georgia came up, put his hand in our soil, found worms, and said this is pretty good. But if you could see the worms in the soil that we were blessed to get and that we are creating now—those worms are like jumping beans, jumping jacks. When you see a worm crawling, that's about the size of n****** — slow moving. But when you put your hand in that new soil, you see worms literally jumping. There's so much life in them because of the life that's in the soil. They are making the soil rich. Ninety percent of the toxicity that's in soil is destroyed by the presence of worms. I'm not talking about soil—I'm talking about you.

You are the earth. You are the foundation of civilization. What has happened is that you have become toxic—a toxic, denatured woman. Have you noticed how the enemy has taken the vitamins, minerals, and proteins out of vegetation. Dr. Alim [Muhammad], our Minister of Health, said a carrot today is not like a carrot 50 years ago. There was life in the food. There was no such thing as a health food store 50 years ago.

Did you know that the earth itself has everything in it that we need? Did you know that when Master Fard Muhammad came to America, the first thing He did was go to the medicine cabinet and take everything that we had in the medicine cabinet and throw it away. If we did that to your medicine cabinet today, you would think that we were the real devil coming in your house to kill you. In reality, your medicine cabinet is killing you. When you look at your medicines and the side effects, you don't know whether you should take the medicine or die with what you got because the side effects are so bad.

Master Fard Muhammad fulfilled what the scripture says (John 10:10), "I came that they may have life and have it more abundantly." A man cannot give you life and give you disease and medicines at the same time. So, He threw the medicine away and said your kitchen is your hospital. Your kitchen. Have you ever heard that before? Some of you who are Muslims may have, but I want my Christian Sisters to remember grandma and great grandma.

They didn't go to college like you and I. We went to college and got stupid-er. They didn't go anywhere but they were in a garden. They studied the nature of what was around them. When we got sick, there wasn't any hospital. They went into the field, picked something, made a tea for us, and we got well. We've lost that power.

## Fulfilling our destinies

Sisters, how can you fulfill your destiny? The Honorable Elijah Muhammad said the woman is your first nurse. She is your first teacher. How many of you have gone to nursing school? That's a heck of a course. What did you have to study to be a nurse? Anatomy, biology chemistry. What do you think a cook is? Some of you hate cooking as though it's demeaning a woman to know how to cook. That's why you have no home today because you don't know how to make a home. The enemy has taken you out of the home and robbed you of the ability to make a home and heal your family through the science of cooking.

You say, "Ain't nobody gonna make me a cook. I have my law degree. I…I…I." Yeah, right—I…I…I don't have peace either because you don't know what to do for a man to keep him when you get him. You don't keep a man by the bed. You keep a man by the wise use of your head. If your head is properly educated, you will know how to take care of a man. You should know how to take care of a man because you want that man to get up in the morning, get out the house, go and make some money, bring that money home, and take care of you and the babies that you produce for him. But if he's tired all the time, sick, and half-broken down, you tell him, "Baby, go to the doctor" and he loads him up with more pills.

God put Adam in a garden and told him to dress the garden. When you wake up in the morning and shower, you will not come out naked. You dress. You cover your nakedness by dressing. God gives you the earth, but then the human being is given a command by God. Adam was to dress the garden. That takes skill. Stupid people can't dress the garden. People who don't know science cannot dress the garden. People who don't know the science of astronomy cannot become great builders. People who don't know the movement of the moon and the seasons won't know when to plant and when to harvest. There's science in life.

God gave this man, Adam, a woman. She was to help him. How many of us know how to help a man? I'm glad it's a few who raised their hands. The others said, "I can't help a man to do nothing." If a man is doing nothing, he doesn't need help. If a man is doing something in accord with his divine nature, he needs a woman who is in accord with her divine nature to help him accomplish what God has put on him to accomplish.

You cannot accomplish that without knowledge. I'm not talking about the education of the world; I'm talking about the acquisition of real knowledge that is practical, that makes you independent of your former slave masters and their children.

We are in the genesis. We're in our beginning and it starts with God making a man. Then the first marriage. I'm sorry, sisters, if two of you love each other. We all should love each other. That's the teaching of Jesus: Love you one another. But he didn't mean it like you're taking it. If two women are married, where is the productivity of re-peopling the planet? Replenish the earth—that is the command of God. "OK, well alright, alright. I'll do my part. I'm going to marry a woman and have a man to get me pregnant. Then, I'll fulfill my obligation." Stop it.

The enemy has made evil fair-seeming. It's not our fault. I'm not here to condemn you or others for what we do of sin because no one in here is holy, including me. But where I stand is holy—not because of me but because of Who is standing with me and backing me up. They are the Holy Ones and Their Holiness covers me.

Preachers should never preach as though we don't have any sin. The Bible says (Romans 3:23), "all have sinned and fall short of the glory of God." And "all" means all. That's why we always look for God's mercy and forgiveness. Each of us is guilty of something. Whatever we're guilty of, it strangles the life force. Doing wrong depletes your energy. If you really want to be powerful, we have to make a decision to do what is right.

## Cain and Abel: Lessons on being productive

Yesterday, the Sisters of the Vanguard presented me and Mother Khadijah with beautiful, beautiful gifts. Your gifts mean more than what you gave me. When God created the earth, the scripture says (Genesis 2:5), "there was no man to till the ground." If God creates a man and there's no man to till the ground, then what's the first great profession? Everything we have on and everything we ate this morning or last night—if there wasn't a farmer, we would have nothing.

Look at what's happening in America. Small farms are being eaten up by big farms. Big farmers are merchants of death. They are feeding us nothing of real value. So, you have to go to the health food store and buy pills. "I've got to have my vitamins." They are fleecing you with food that has no value in the supermarket, fleecing you with pills that have some value but now you're full of disease—diabetes, heart trouble, and cancer. We are a sick people. We're sick because we have depended on our enemy to take care of us.

"There was no man to till the ground." Tilling means to farm, work, plow, dig, fertilize, cultivate a crop, plant, raise, tend, bring on, and produce. God wants us to be productive of what you need to sustain and maintain your life—food, clothing, and shelter. Who's doing that for us? Somebody else.

What kind of woman are you that you're not making your children to see the value of the earth and making productive men rather than a bunch of dependent men who walk around with a degree on the wall that means nothing because they produce nothing.

If you are going to dress the garden, if you are going to till the land, let's look at Cain and Abel. Marriage produced two children for Adam. Cain was the eldest child. The Bible said he was a tiller of the ground. Isn't that what God wanted—somebody to farm? Then Abel was born.

When they matured, Abel was raising sheep. Cain was tilling the ground. At a certain point, Cain presented the crop to the Lord. The Bible says (Genesis 4:5) that God did not respect Cain's offering. I find that very hard to believe and I would like, in my own humble way, to correct the way the scripture is phrased.

God would not say He didn't have someone to till the ground when Adam produced a son who was able to till the ground and worked hard to till the ground to produce a crop for God. Why wouldn't God respect his effort? It's not that God didn't respect his effort, but He found more favor in Abel's offering of the firstling of a sheep, a little lamb.

When it looked like God accepted a lamb and seemed to reject his hard work, Cain's face fell. His countenance dropped. He became angry. When you make a presentation and it appears that your presentation has no value in the eyes of those to whom you presented, it does something to your spirit. Your face drops. Your countenance falls. Sometimes you become angry and embittered.

God asked Cain, "Why has your countenance fallen? Why are you angry?" If Cain had spoken up and said, "You made me till the ground. Why didn't you accept my work? I did the work." Farming is hard. Ask the Brothers at the farm how hard they work to produce the crops that we're producing. That's no lightweight thing. There's sweat from your brow to produce a crop.

I'm sure God respected that work and sweat, but God had something else in mind that Cain didn't question him about. Sometimes when you're angry and embittered, you have to raise questions because it could be that nobody is rejecting you but they see something that maybe you didn't see.

Why did God accept a lamb and appear to reject the sweat of Cain to produce a crop? It is because at the end of the world that Adam's rebellion produced, a lamb-like human being would come to birth. Through that Lamb of God, the sins of the world would be taken away. Through that Lamb of God, man would once again be reconciled to God. God wasn't putting Cain down, but He saw so far into the future that He took Abel's lamb as a sign of His acceptance of that Lamb that would come at the end of the world of evil.

## Preparing our future

In our work today, women, as the helper of God, you must study science. You must study chemistry. You cannot nurse your home, children, and husband with a pork chop, McDonald's, or crazy fried food. You must know the value of what you're putting in your mouth and what you're putting in the mouths of your children. When you go to the store to buy food, you have to know what you're looking for.

My mother used to take me shopping with her and I would watch my mother turn fruit over and turn vegetables over, check it out, take this one, and leave that one. She'd go to the meat counter and have them bring the meat out so she could look at it. Today, it's all packaged. It looks so nice. The orange is so orange. The apple is so red. You don't know that they are gassing and coloring them to make them look that way. If you don't know the value of the land, then you'll be in the supermarket, dying from the mess that they feed you because you don't know any better. When you know better, you are expected to do better.

Sisters, a class has been set up, first to teach us sewing. Look at the clothes you have on. How much did an inferior garment cost you? You cannot even dress your girl children decently. Their little navels are out wearing short clothing. It's very sickening. You take it because when you shop at these stores, there's nothing decent there to buy.

There's nothing decent there to cover yourself because the enemy doesn't want you covered. The enemy wants your man to be a dog. How are you going to prepare a future for your girls and yourself if you don't know how to take a pattern and make something to style yourself in a beautiful way. You can do that, but you don't want to do that because you think that's beneath you—lawyer, doctor, accountant.

That's not beneath you. When you dress in your suit with tight pants and go downtown, you know what that White man is saying to you. He's trying to grope you and do all kinds of things. He wouldn't grope you dressed like this. He'll get messed up, not only will these [pointing to Vanguard] whip his behind, but we'll come behind them and he'll have no behind left.

## Vanguard gifts presented to Minister Farrakhan

Sister Sandy [National Captain of the M.G.T.-G.C.C.], would you come forward for a minute please. Bring me the first things that the Sisters gave me. This is the presentation that the Sisters made. The Jr. M.G.T. Vanguard made their own cookbook. If you look in their cookbook, you will find that they know something about chemistry. They chose foods that enrich the body, stimulate the mind, and create more energy. That's a beautiful gift.

We're starting off now as we used to train women when I was a youngster. Women had to learn the art of homemaking. Even if you had a college course, you still had to know how to make a home, and to make a home you had to know something about cooking. That's lost now. It's Sara Lee—whoever that is.

Someone cooking for us, but you don't even know what their kitchen looks like. You don't know whether they blew their nose and shook it in the pot. I'm serious. You have some nasty, dirty people on television showing you how to cook. I saw one woman lick a utensil and then put it back in the pot and put her hand in the pot. In our kitchen, you must be clean. In our kitchen, you must wear a hairnet because we don't want to eat your hair [Asian weave] in our plate.

There's nothing wrong with cooking. Try to learn. Learn the best foods to eat, how to prepare them, and give yourself health. Don't spend money on fine things and neglect good foods. Good food for you and good food for your children.

Never send your children to school with an empty stomach. Never. Feed your children properly before you send them to school. Prepare a healthy meal for them when they come home. This is your duty as a woman. If you don't do it, you're shortchanging your children, you're shortchanging yourself, and you're shortchanging our future as a people. Next? Sister Sandy, what is in this?

*Sister Sandy: It's handcrafted, natural soap, detergent, soy candles that burn toxin free, and towels that were embroidered in monogram by the M.G.T. and G.C.C. Vanguard.*

Minister Farrakhan: From the earth, you produce industry. Here's young girls making soap. We know what's in this soap because we made it. And it looks good, too.

*Sister Sandy: There's also bath salts in there made from Dead Sea salt.*

Minister Farrakhan: Dead Sea salt—it's good for mentally dead people (smile).

*Sister Sandy: Sister Tracy out of Miami trained the Vanguard and some junior M.G.T. Vanguard to do this project.*

Minister Farrakhan: We've lost this ability—handcrafts, needlecrafts. You've lost it. Grandma knew how to do this. They made quilts that covered our bodies. They made sweaters. They made things with their hands.

      You have lost that art and you must get it again because we are going to do business from farms, creating what we call agribusiness. Next, please. These are young women, they're busy. Thank you, M.G.T. for teaching our young women this.

*Sister Sandy: This is another product made by the M.G.T. -G.C.C. Vanguard. It is a throw blanket, a pillow for the head, and a lap pillow made from raw silk. The M.G.T. Vanguard sewed the pillows by hand and used a sewing machine to sew the blanket.*

Minister Farrakhan: Do you know how the Jews got rich? We were on the farms picking cotton. We picked that cotton. Cotton yesterday was like oil is today. We picked that cotton. They turned the cotton into lint and the lint into cloth. Their brothers and sisters in the north became masters of the needle trades.

So when we needed a blanket, the Jewish man downtown sold you a blanket. If you needed a pillowcase or a sheet, you didn't make the pillowcase or the sheet. You just picked the cotton out of which White folks made the sheet—and we were in the factory working for them. Why can't we do that for ourselves? if we don't create industry, we will always be dependent on someone else to do for us what we could do for ourselves. What's next?

This is a little booklet called, "How to Take Care of Your Husband." These are courses that we take as women in the class but that doesn't mean it stops there. These Sisters are learning so much wisdom. Their divine and moral character is becoming more and more visible. We are proud of your effort. We hope our women— Christian, Muslim, Jewish, or nationalists—we must go back to creating, production and industry. But it all has to start from the ownership of land. Do you agree?

What's next? That's it. Thank you, Sister Sandy. You're doing a wonderful, wonderful job. Thank you.

## A word to men

I should say a word to men. If what I said hurt you as a man, that was not my intention. My intention was for us, as men, to see the value of any woman in our lives. My intention was to tell these young ones—some of them 12, 14, just growing into a young woman; some 17, 18, 19, 20—I want them to know how valuable they are so that when men hit on them, they will know how to resist.

Sisters, fasting is prescribed in the Bible and Qur'an. To take a day when you say I'm not going to eat today, and you know you need food to keep going. If you learn how to fast, you're beginning to discipline your appetites. Through learning how to fast, when your hormones become active and you're disturbed in a biological way, you can still manage to control your appetites. Learn how to fast but before that prayer.

Prayer, the remembrance of God, is the greatest force in the restraining of the doing of evil. Prayer charity, and fasting—the struggle with yourself. If you would do that, in a short while you will be able to be examples to our beautiful women out there. We have a great people out there who are suffering drugs and all the things that we've been through. God is blessing us to conquer our own weaknesses so we can help others master their weaknesses. That's your duty. That's your job.

For now, put a man out of your mind. That's not necessary right now. What is necessary is that you cultivate yourself as a woman in the character of Divine. You are not man's woman. You are the woman of God. He uses you in a co-creative work of creating the human beings that will make a better world for God.

Your womb is sacred. No man should have access to that channel if he's not a God-fearing man who loves God. Because he loves God, he will love you. From the love of God that both of you have, you will produce a child, like Jesus who Mary produced. We don't have to have a lot of devils coming out of your womb. We can produce Jesus over and over and over and over again if we devote our womb to God.

Brothers, when you have a woman like that, the Honorable Elijah Muhammad said when you produce a crop, you kill the insects and things that would destroy your crop. You pull up the weeds that will choke out your crop. If someone tried to steal your crop, you're justified in using your shotgun. How much more valuable are our women? The Honorable Elijah Muhammad said no nation on earth will ever respect us until we can prove that we love and respect our women. Then, they'll know that we respect ourselves because she's a part of us.

No good man will ever beat a woman. No good man will be violent to a woman. "I have a woman. She mouths off on me." So what? if you learn how to handle yourself, God will help you handle your woman. Sisters, you don't like that word "control," but you are out of control. You are out of control because there's no regulation. There's no regulator. There are no regulations that you are submitting to that brings you under divine control.

A man that's like we are, doesn't know how to control you. I know you resent even the talk of that. Remember the vows when you got married: "Will you honor and obey?" They just wrote that right out. "I'm not going to obey that fool." If he's a fool, what are you doing with him? if you can't respect him enough to obey him, what do you have him for? You should always want a man who proves to you he's wise enough, intelligent enough, and careful enough to guide you; and he's respectful enough to listen to truth coming out of your mouth when he's in error. That is the type of man that you want in your life.

Brothers, we must stop this foolishness of allowing anyone to come into our neighborhood and take our women. The White man has sense. He'll kill you if he sees you with his woman; he used to. Today he'll give her to you. And we're really killing White folks without a gun because the heavy charge that the Black man is shooting, that fellow is going off the planet with these half-white babies coming in the world. I'm serious. He's dying a natural death.

If you love your woman, we don't like you out all hours of the night. What are you out there for? What kind of man are you or me or us that our women can hang out all night long. You don't even ask her where she's been. "I've been where I've been." Wait a minute, Sisters. You have children or one day when you have children, you are going to want to regulate their coming and going. You're going to look at who they're bring to your house as their friends and you will tell them, "No, no, no, no, no, no, not that one."

If you can regulate the affairs of your children, why don't we, as men, let God regulate our affairs; then we regulate the affairs of our house, so God is ruling the house. Brothers, we're going to have to be willing to fight, to kill, to die protecting our woman. "Did you say kill?" That's exactly what I said. Look at the men in jail right now for killing someone over you but you weren't worthy. But if you're going to try to be righteous, then you're worthy for us to fight for you, die for you, and kill anyone that wants to mess with you, rape you, and destroy your value.

If that doesn't please you, you say, "I was doing alright until that man said kill. I thought they were righteous people." A righteous person will kill in defense of righteousness. You've been made a silly people. "We shouldn't hate anybody. Hate destroys the hater." Listen to your stupid self. You let the White man teach you that. "We have to love everybody." Who said that? Show me in the Bible where God told you to love everybody.

What caused God to kill and flood all those people in the days of Noah? Did he love the wicked? No. He killed the wicked. He also threatened, as it was in the days of Noah, so shall it be at the Coming of the Son of Man. Did He love the homosexuals in Sodom and Gomorrah? What did He do? He killed them. Not even a blade of grass grows today in Sodom and Gomorrah. Did He love Pharoah? What did He do? He killed Pharoah. If you don't have killing in you, then you don't have God in you.

Thank you for listening. *As-Salaam Alaikum.*

# ABOUT
# THE FINAL CALL FOUNDATION

Final Call Foundation

The Final Call Foundation was established in 2021 with the purpose to support raising awareness, preserving, researching, and amplifying the public works and personal history of the Honorable Minister Louis Farrakhan in the uplift of all humanity.

Follow us:  ❶ 📷  @finalcallfoundation
            🐦  @FCFcharity

Visit The Final Call Foundation Amazon Author Pages:
www.amazon.com/author/finalcallfoundationhmlf
www.amazon.com/author/finalcallfoundation

## **Upcoming Titles**

**The Time and What Must Be Done**
**Volumes 1 & 2**
*A series of weekly broadcast messages delivered by the Honorable Minister Louis Farrakhan from January 2013 to February 2014.*

# AVAILABLE TITLES

**Sarah: Five Notes on a Woman's Prayer over Her Pregnancy**

**A Demonstration of Love**

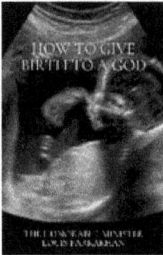

**How To Give Birth To A God**

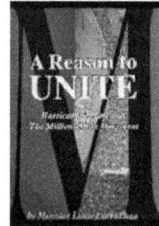

**A Reason to Unite**
Hurricane Katrina and the Millions More Movement

**A Saviour is Born for the Black Man and Woman of America**

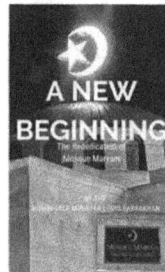

**A New Beginning**
The Rededication of Mosque Maryam

# ABOUT THE EDITOR

Dora Muhammad is an artist, author, and advocate. She served as editor-in-chief of *The Final Call* Newspaper from 2003-2006. In 2010, she founded The AWARE Project, a multimedia vehicle for advocacy on issues relative to women's awareness, engagement, rights, empowerment, and advancement. She earned a Bachelor of Arts in Journalism and Documentary Photography, with a concentration in Magazine Production and completed her photography thesis at Dartington School of the Arts in Devon, England. She worked as an arts administrator for Autograph-ABP (Association of Black Photographers) while studying International Law and Human Rights at the University of London. Dora earned her Master of Public Administration and has extensive work in government relations and public policy formation. A daughter of Indo-Caribbean immigrant parents, Dora is a native New Yorker who resides in Northern Virginia. She currently serves as the executive director of The Final Call Foundation.

Visit the Dora Muhammad and AWARE Project Amazon Author Pages for a catalog of her books.

www.ingramcontent.com/pod-product-compliance
Lightning Source LLC
Chambersburg PA
CBHW052134270326
41930CB00012B/2875